In Search of My Father

To Ellen & Paul

With warm wishes

Paul

Paul Drexler

25 - 12 - 15

*In loving memory of my beloved parents Eugen
and Helen Drexler.*

*To the love of my life, my wife Diane.
To our beautiful daughters Julie and Michelle.*

*And to the one and a half million innocent children
killed in the Holocaust.*

In Search of My Father

My Father

The journey of a child Holocaust survivor

JoJo
PUBLISHING

Paul Drexler

In Search of My Father : The journey of a child Holocaust survivor

By Paul Drexler
Second edition 2010
Published by JoJo Publishing

First Published in 2006
© Paul Drexler 2006

'Yarra's Edge'
2203/80 Lorimer Street
Docklands VIC 3008
Australia

Email: jo-media@bigpond.net.au or visit www.jojopublishing.com

National Library of Australia
Cataloguing-in-Publication data
                Drexler, Eugen.
                Drexler, Paul.
                Jewish children in the Holocaust--Slovakia--Biography.
                Jews--Australia--Biography.
                World War, 1939-1945--Personal narratives, Jewish.

                ISBN 9780980518511 (pbk.)

                940.5318092

Designer / typesetter: Rob Ryan @ Z Design Media
Printed in Singapore by Hobee Printers

CONTENTS

ACKNOWLEDGEMENTS

This book could not have been written without the encouragement and assistance of my wife Diane. She eased my burden as I relived the painful experiences of the past and travelled the journey with me.

I thank our daughters, Julie and Michelle, for their assistance with research and their many positive suggestions, which have enhanced my writing.

I am indebted to my editor, Charlotte Strong, for her guidance and meticulous attention to detail.

Special thanks to Dr Paul O'Shea and Professor Konrad Kwiet for their invaluable advice and assistance with historical research.

To our extended family and good friends, my sincere thanks for your consistent support and goodwill throughout my writing.

FOREWORD

The annihilation of human life, the destruction of family ties and the extinction of entire communities were the legacy of the Holocaust – the state-sanctioned murder of six million European Jews. The victims perished in ghettos, camps and sealed freight cars. Some two million were shot 'in the open' – at the outskirts of villages, in secluded forest areas or occasionally on beaches. More than three million were put to death in mobile or stationary gassing installations. Unprecedented in history, the heinous crimes perpetrated defied human imagination. They also did not permit a burial according to Jewish law. Cemeteries were replaced by killing fields, which served as burial sites. The mass graves were levelled. With the passage of time the layers of corpses decomposed and disintegrated, leaving behind human remains intermingled with a few personal belongings of victims and bullets fired by perpetrators. Most of those murdered by poison gas were cremated and their ashes dispersed, in water or soil.

Such genocidal campaigns did not require the recording of the names of victims. As a rule, only numbers were reported. The secrecy surrounding the killings gave rise to problems of religious observance and remembrance for the descendants. As an ancient custom dictates, Jews are compelled to commemorate the Yahrzeit and to recite Kaddish – the traditional prayer of mourning for the deceased. After liberation, the few survivors embarked on long journeys to rebuild their shattered lives. All of them were searching for missing family members and friends.

For Paul Drexler, a child survivor, this search has only just come to an end. Not long ago he uncovered the date and the place of the murder of his beloved father. His autobiographical account covers a lifespan of more than sixty years. It brings Holocaust history, trauma and memory together by reconstructing the journey back into the past. His recollections are a compelling, intriguing piece of writing.

At the start are the memories of a happy childhood spent in rural Slovakia. Indelible are the images of the idyllic family home, loving caring parents and extensive family ties, vignettes of a Jewish world in which the Drexlers had found a sound economic existence and had enjoyed the achievements of social integration and acculturation. Slovak anti-Semites, a dominant force in the Tiso regime, superseded by the German executioners of the 'Final Solution', destroyed the very foundation of this Jewish world in which the family had felt at home. In autumn 1944, at the age of six, Paul Drexler experienced the forced separation from his father.

What follows are months of suffering and survival. His recollections of this time follow a clear chronological sequence: escape with his mother into hiding, arrest, incarceration in the transit camp of Sered, deportation, life and liberation in Theresienstadt. Like other survivors, Paul and his mother, upon their return home, were greeted by neighbours with surprise, suspicion and hostility. Paul recalls the struggle to come to terms with feelings of isolation and loss and the decision to seek sanctuary in Australia. Unforgotten are certain experiences en route to the Antipodes and upon arrival in the metropolis of Sydney. However, he portrays in greater detail the social setting of his upbringing. His reflections lead the reader into a hitherto largely unexplored milieu of Holocaust survivors and their children. In Paul Drexler's case, the necessity felt by his mother to place her son in a boarding home, freeing her up to establish a modest economic base, had a deep impact on his formative years. These recollections bear witness to the energy, ambition and resourcefulness of a child survivor to firmly establish himself in his newly adopted home country. Like many other refugees, he succeeded in achieving this. Some years passed before integration and acculturation were completed.

As a loyal Australian citizen and proud Australian Jew he embarked on a successful professional and social career. A happy marriage paved the way to a fulfilled family life and – as in the past – to the establishment of new extensive family ties reaching across continents.

Yet, in this success story there are the scars of traumatic experiences, scars that do not disappear. The questions surrounding his father's disappearance remained unresolved. Fifteen years ago the prevailing wall of silence was gradually broken down. Paul Drexler began to tell his story – first at the Emanuel School, then to the Spielberg Foundation and finally as a guide at the Sydney Jewish Museum.

The more he served as a living witness of the Holocaust the stronger his desire to uncover the fate of his father. The efforts undertaken with the historical and archival studies, the trips to memorial sites and places of the past, were not in vain.

Paul's father fell victim to the last great massacre of the Nazi Regime, a tragedy that for many years remained a forgotten chapter of the Holocaust. Together with other inmates from various concentration camps he was sent on a death march, which ended at Lübeck Bay on the Baltic Sea in Northern Germany. For the rest of his life Paul Drexler lives with the knowledge of the date and place of the murder of his father. This now allows him – after more than sixty years – to commemorate the correct Yahrzeit and to recite Kaddish.

Konrad Kwiet

Adjunct Professor in Jewish Studies and Roth Lecturer in Holocaust Studies University of Sydney, Resident Historian Sydney Jewish Museum

CHAPTER

I

IN THE BEGINNING

'Honour thy Father...'

On 8 May 2005, the sixtieth anniversary of VE Day: the surrender of Germany, I sat at my writing desk, remembering. On that day in 1945 I was a skinny, half-starved seven year old boy liberated from a Nazi camp in Czechoslovakia. With me were my mother and grandmothers. None of us had any idea where my father was. On that mid-spring day, I became, like so many other Jews across Europe, a survivor. My mother and I went home. But, my father never did.

Years later I began searching for the man known as Eugen Drexler – my father. The journey to find him began in no set way; all I can say is that the story came together almost of its own accord. And it started in 1996 with a trip I never thought I would make. At the end of this journey, I had travelled from Australia to places I never imagined I would see or feel, and I had learnt the truth about my father's tragic death.

September 1996. The Lauda Air 777 was taking off from Sydney International Airport. Peering through the window at the glistening waters of Sydney Harbour below, my thoughts were apprehensively focused on my birthplace in Czechoslovakia. I was taking my family: my wife, Diane and my daughters, Julie and Michelle, back to the village of Špačince in the Slovak Republic that I had left as a nine year old child. I had never expected to return.

I felt a pain in the pit of my stomach as the plane climbed higher. I held Diane's hand tightly. My mind was awash with questions left unanswered about my experiences during the Holocaust. I needed confirmation. I needed to know the truth.

Other than to Diane and my closest friends, I had always been reluctant to speak openly about my parents and my own experiences during the Holocaust. It was a chapter in my life that I had wanted to forget. I did not want to bring further attention to myself – I just wanted to move on with my life and not dwell on the past.

That was until Julie, our elder daughter, at 13 years of age, studied the Holocaust in Jewish Studies at the Emanuel School, Randwick. Julie had often asked me why I only had one picture of my late father; why I didn't have pictures of myself as a child with my parents and my grandparents; why I had no pictures of myself at kindergarten, primary school or birthday parties when we had so many pictures of her and her younger sister around our home. While she was growing up, I told Julie briefly about my past and the reasons why there were no photographs but I thought it was too early in her life to expose her to the horror of the Holocaust.

In 1994, the same year that Julie was studying the Holocaust, a travelling exhibition from Prague of children's paintings from the former Theresienstadt ghetto/concentration camp came to Sydney. Her year 8 teacher, Benny Kaplinski, took the opportunity of taking the class to see it. The next day Julie mentioned to Benny that I was a child survivor of Theresienstadt. He telephoned me and asked me if I would speak to the class about it. I surprised myself by saying yes.

One week later I stood in front of two classes of fresh-faced boys and girls who were eager to know more about my life. I spoke for about thirty minutes and showed them some of my possessions from when I was in Theresienstadt in 1944–45. When I had finished, I thanked the class and their teacher for giving me the opportunity to speak in public for the first time. I was overcome by a sense of achievement; I felt good. I had broken the silence of fifty years.

But by the time I reached my car I was in tears. I could not hold them in as the memories came flooding back to me.

When I got home, I told Diane what had happened at the school. That was when she told me that it had always been her hope that I would document my childhood experience of the Holocaust, so that our daughters would have a true record of their father's life and understand their own genealogical link to the Holocaust. Diane encouraged me to open up – to put my memories down on paper. So that evening I began writing all the facts that I could remember. This was the beginning of a writing process that would go on for several years.

Some time after this, we discovered that the Steven Spielberg Shoah Foundation was seeking Holocaust survivors to be interviewed for a video archive. Film director Steven Spielberg had established the foundation following the production of his film *Schindler's List*, to preserve the testimony of Holocaust survivors for future generations. Diane encouraged me to do an interview, which I did in March 1995. During the three-hour session, I was surprised that I remembered so many facts of my family's life in the Holocaust and my journey to Australia. In front of the camera, my memories flowed.

Later the same month we visited Israel for the first time. Yad Vashem, The Holocaust Martyrs' and Heroes' Memorial made great impressions on Julie and Michelle. For me the visit was distressing. Memories of the Holocaust flooded my mind. I found myself in a daze. I thought back fifty years to the last time I had seen my father. I had always wondered what had happened to him and how he had died. Since I became a father myself, I had never felt complete not knowing the truth of his death.

On our return home and before we unpacked our luggage, I knew in my heart that I had to return to my birthplace in Slovakia. My strength and inspiration came from Diane, Julie and Michelle. They gave me tremendous support and encouraged me to make the journey and to take them with me so that together we could retrace my life.

We arrived in Bratislava, the capital of Slovakia, at midday on September 25 1996 and checked into the Forum Hotel, opposite the President's Palace in the middle of the city. The hotel provided us with a car and a driver. Our forty year old driver Stefan had greying-blonde hair and was immaculately dressed in a brown sports jacket and cream slacks. He looked more like a business executive than a chauffeur. He spoke sufficient English to hold a pleasant conversation.

We left the next day for the small village of Špačince, where I was born. I had done plenty of research in the months leading up to our departure as I needed to be sure that Špačince was still in existence. The Slovak Embassy in Canberra had confirmed that it was, and sent me a map.

Now that I knew the village still existed, I allowed myself to wonder if the house in which I was born was still standing. In my mind I had a clear picture of my childhood home. It was situated on a corner of the main street into Špačince. I remembered that the house itself could not be seen from the road because it was behind a high concrete fence with two heavy brown metal gates.

As we got closer, my heart began to beat faster and faster and I felt a gripping anxiety take hold. We drove down a modern four-lane highway, which had been constructed during the communist era and led directly into Špačince. There was a tremendous change in the landscape since I last saw it in 1946. The large farmhouses with thatched roofs were gone. Small semi-detached cottages replaced them; it was now more like a scene from an English town than the Špačince I remembered. We drove through the streets but I couldn't see our old property. I was feeling very distressed.

There were only a few people on the streets. Some

young schoolchildren waved to us from their school-yard. This was not the old village that I had left fifty years ago.

My anxiety increased and I found breathing difficult. But my determination to find the house was unwavering.

I remembered that the land on which my family home stood extended down a hill towards a creek, and there was a small bridge over the creek on the roadway leading to the house. Diane remembered that we had passed a creek earlier. We then drove in a circle until we found it again, and a small bridge over the roadway. We drove up the small hill; then turned right, stopped and got out of the car.

I looked across the road and there, near the corner, was a high concrete fence with a brown metal gate. 'That is the house!' I exclaimed.

I explained to Julie and Michelle that there used to be a courtyard leading to the front door that opened into a very spacious kitchen. In the courtyard before the front door was a well with a pump from which we got our fresh water.

As we surveyed the scene before us, a small red car stopped in front of the gate, and a stocky man in a grey suit got out and opened the gate. He drove the car into a very overgrown courtyard and parked it in front of the main door. The house was now visible. It was in a very dilapidated condition. The most modern house in Špačince when I was born in 1938 was now the oldest in the village.

We quickly crossed the street and walked through the gate towards the man, who looked somewhat puzzled. My Slovak was very limited so I spoke to the man in German.

He did not understand. Fortunately, Stefan came to my rescue. He told the man that we were visiting from Australia and that I had been born in the house and lived there as a small child. The man smiled broadly and told Stefan that his father purchased the house from a Jewish woman at the end of the war. That was my mother. He further elaborated that he grew up in the house and that his family had lived there for many years. But the house was now only used for storage.

The man was quite friendly and invited us to come inside. As I walked towards the front door I came across the well. It was totally overgrown with vines, but after fifty years it was still there.

We entered the kitchen; it was full of old furniture, picture frames and utensils. On the right hand wall was a cavity where the large stove originally stood – the powerhouse of the kitchen. As I looked around, tears that I could not hold back streamed down my face.

I closed my eyes and remembered the large stove. A huge pot sat on the burner, the lid not fully closed and steam rising. The aroma was delightful; it must be chicken soup. A square table with four chairs stood in the middle of the kitchen. To the right was a door leading to the dining and living rooms and to the left was the main bedroom. This was the house in which I was born at three o'clock in the morning on 29 June 1938. The local midwife had assisted my birth. I was named Pavel Drexler and given the nickname of Palko. I was the first and only son of Eugen and Helen Drexler.

'PEACE IN OUR TIME'

The democracy of Czechoslovakia was established after the collapse of the Austro-Hungarian Empire at the end of World War I. The new republic, comprised of the states of Bohemia, Moravia and Slovakia, was officially recognised as Czechoslovakia in September 1919, with Thomas Masaryk as President and Eduard Benes as his deputy. The republic was distinguished by its stability and experienced domestic prosperity throughout the 1920s and early 30s.

Three months after my birth, on 30 September 1938, the British Prime Minister Neville Chamberlain returned to England after attending the Munich Conference, at which the Munich Agreement was signed by Chamberlain, Hitler, Mussolini and Daladier. Another agreement was also signed in Munich. In front of a jubilant crowd in West London, Chamberlain waved a piece of paper signed by both himself and Adolf Hitler on the day before, that stated Hitler's intention never to go to war with Britain again. Chamberlain famously declared the agreement as signalling 'peace in our time'. While Britain celebrated what it thought was an averted war, the model democracy of Czechoslovakia had effectively been destroyed by the signing of the Munich Agreement, which ceded the Sudetenland of Czechoslovakia to Germany. 'Peace in our time' would not be the outcome.

In 1935 Eduard Benes had succeeded Masaryk as President of Czechoslovakia. However, he considered the Munich Agreement of 1938 a grave betrayal and resigned from office in October of that year. He fled to London. Emil Hacha succeeded him as President, although a year later in September 1939 Benes established a government-in-exile in London.

Chamberlain hoped that the offering up of Czechoslovakia to Germany would appease Hitler's territorial ambitions. He was wrong and my family, along with millions of others, would pay the price.

On 15 March 1939 Hitler marched into Prague and created the Reichprotectorate of Bohemia and Moravia. On the day before, the newly formed state of Slovakia, led by Josef Tiso, had gained nominal independence as a satellite state closely allied with Germany.

Tiso was a nationalist Catholic priest who in 1939 had become President of the Slovak People's Party of Hlinka (more commonly known as the Ludaks), after the death of the party's anti-Semitic nationalist leader and founder Father Andrej Hlinka. Tiso promoted a radical order based on Catholicism and espoused an ideology of nationalism, anti-communism and anti-Semitism. His prime minister, Dr Vojtech Tuka, was even more extreme. Soon after Slovakia's proclamation of independence, the Hlinka Guard, a body similar in character to the SS, began terrorising and killing Jews.

Tiso ordered all Jews out of the Slovak economy and 'aryanised' Jewish property. Slovak forces carried out house-to-house confiscations of personal property including jewellery, silver and antiques.

In 1941, when Slovak troops joined the Nazi war effort, the pace of anti-Jewish legislation quickened. Young Jews were drafted into forced labour. Now, all Jews were forced to wear armbands, marked with the yellow Star of David.

The Tiso government actively supported the idea of deporting all Jews. At the secret 1942 Wannsee Conference in Berlin, where plans for the Final Solution were discussed, participants were told, 'Slovak cooperation seemed assured'.

But when the Nazis asked for twenty thousand young Jews 'to build new Jewish settlements', the Slovak government panicked, not because it worried about the fate of its Jews, but because it feared being left with the old and sick. As a solution to this perceived problem, Tiso demanded the entire Slovak Jewish community be deported – never to be returned. The Nazis agreed on condition the Slovak government pay a fee of 500 Reichsmark per deported Jew for 'vocational retraining'. On 23 June 1942, Tiso, drawing on confiscated Jewish assets, paid Berlin its requested fee.

According to the census of 15 December 1940, there were about 90,000 Jews in Slovakia. Between March and October 1942, almost 60,000 Jews were herded by local ethnic Germans and members of the Hlinka Guard onto trains and transported to the Polish border, where

German guards took over for the final destinations: 19 transports to Auschwitz and 38 transports to Majdanek and Lublin region.

In 1942, Slovak Jews whose services were considered an economic necessity escaped deportation under a government exemption approved by Tiso. Since my father was needed for his expertise in the wheat industry, this exemption allowed my family to stay in Slovakia for a while longer. My father was granted a white identity card, which exempted him and our family from some limitations imposed on the rights of the Jews. For example, he was still allowed to advise wheat farmers and continue trading on behalf of them, as this was important for the economy.

Being given this white identity card was like being given air to breathe. Not only was it a work permit, but also, from the spring of 1942, it kept the holders, their wives and children and both sets of parents excluded from deportation to the death camps.

HAPPY CHILDHOOD

In 1943 in Špačince I was an ordinary, secure, five year old boy, unaware of the dangerous times we were living in and ignorant of the pressure my parents were under. I recall spending my days playing with children from the village and being absorbed by all the activity on our property.

Attached to our house was a small apartment where my paternal grandmother, Regina, lived. Behind the apartment was a vacant block of land on which we had plum trees growing. Further down the property were the stables that housed four horses and a small dairy shed with cows. I remember the night when my father was woken up by an employee shouting 'get the vet, get the vet'. One of the cows was giving birth.

Next to the dairy shed was another shed with two coaches, and behind these buildings was a small patch of land where we grew potatoes. Beyond this was a narrow creek where my father took me to paddle, his strong arms holding my five year old frame up so that I didn't fall into the deep water.

There was a separate entrance gate to our property opposite the stables. A big white Alsatian guarded the gate. In addition to horses and cows, we also reared chickens, ducks and a few turkeys for our own use. Our house was close to the corner of the main street. A storage building for wheat stood on the actual corner.

Špačince was a small agricultural village, seven kilometres north of Trnava in Slovakia. My father, Eugen (known as Jeno to his family and friends), was born in Špačince, as was his father, Gabriel, and his grandfather, Jacob. Špačince was home to at least four generations of Drexlers.

Wheat was the most important commodity grown in Slovakia and my family had been involved in the wheat industry for many years.

My father was born on 26 January 1900. He began his career in wheat at age 14, when his father, Gabriel, became ill and was unable to work. My father became the breadwinner for his parents, three brothers and one sister. His mother (my grandmother) Regina had a small grocery shop in the village from which she was able to contribute towards the upkeep of the family.

Despite humble beginnings as a wheat farmer, my father took the initiative to study the wheat industry in-depth and became an expert. Eventually he represented all the wheat farmers in the Špačince district and travelled frequently to various cities to sell the grain at the grain exchanges to flour millers. My father was respected by the farmers for the technical assistance he provided them for their betterment. He became popular because of his patience and understanding, and sense of fairness.

My mother Helen (known as Loncy to the family and friends) was born on 26 January 1906 in Trnava. She was the youngest of seven children. Her parents were Abraham and Maria Weiss. After leaving school she was employed as a sales assistant in a textile shop in Trnava. My mother had a vivacious personality and made friends easily. Soon she became a close friend of the Manheims, owners of the textile shop.

My mother's oldest brother Arnold and his wife Josephine lived in Vienna, along with her sisters Natalie and Bertha and their husbands Ludwig and Adolf. From the time my mother turned seventeen she spent many weekends in Vienna enjoying opera, concerts and plays together with her brother and sisters.

My parents, Loncy and Jeno, met through mutual friends in 1930. Their friendship grew stronger and it was not long before they were engaged. Their marriage took place on 15 March 1931 in the Status Quo Temple, an orthodox synagogue, in Trnava.

After the wedding, my mother left her family home in Trnava to settle in Špačince with my father. By this time she had become the only child of Maria and Abraham Weiss still living at home. Her much older siblings had migrated to the United States about ten years earlier. Sisters Rose and Erna settled in Wisconsin while Hermine chose New York. Arnold and Josephine left Vienna for Wisconsin in 1930. My mother's two remaining sisters, Bertha and Natalie, together with their husbands, continued living in Vienna.

Although only seven kilometres away from Trnava, the small village of Špačince was a very different world. Trnava, a walled town, is the oldest town in Slovakia. It is fifty kilometres northeast of Bratislava and was one of Hungary's biggest and wealthiest towns by the

13th century, when the first brick fortifications were built. After the Turkish victory in 1526 the archbishops of Esztergom transferred their seat to Trnava and other Catholic orders followed, building churches, monasteries, schools and a Jesuit university. Trnava became known as 'the Slovak Rome'.

The Turks were gradually pushed back and in 1777 Empress Maria Teresa had the entire university moved to Buda. In 1782 Emperor Josef II dissolved the monasteries and moved the Hungarian capital from Bratislava back to Buda. The power in Trnava was gone; only the churches remained. Slovak National Revival followed and in 1792 the printing of books in the newly codified Slovak language began.

The streets of Trnava were cobbled. There were eleven churches and two synagogues, a university, a well-known chocolate factory and other small industries.

My mother lived at 28 Kapitulska Ulica. She always talked about the Yeshiva situated in her street, with its many bearded students in their black coats studying the Talmud. Trnava was a good place to live and work. Elegant shops lined the main retail street, Hlavna Ulica, with the biggest being a Bata shoe outlet. The town boasted three large movie houses as well as a live theatre and concert hall and several coffee houses.

Shortly after the death of my paternal grandfather Gabriel in 1938, my parents moved to a new house in Špačince. My paternal grandmother, Regina, moved into the apartment attached to the house. The old family home in Špačince, further along the main road, was sold, along with Regina's grocery shop. My father had a new shop built adjacent to our house with the entrance in the street around the corner.

My grandmother's shop ceased trading and was boarded up from the inside when Jews were no longer allowed to carry on business. My memory of the shop is when my mother used it as a large pantry for storing her homemade pickles, jams and preserved peaches and pears. A wonderful aroma came from the rail over the counter where she hung the salamis and smoked meats.

Three years before I was born my mother gave birth to a beautiful girl, whom my parents named Eve. In the photo my mother showed me, Eve had lovely curly brown hair. Eve died before she reached two years of age. Throughout my early years my mother often spoke about Eve and how old she would have been. Being so young I did not realise the impact Eve's death had on my mother. As I do not know where Eve is buried, I have put her name before mine on my mother's tombstone, to keep her memory alive.

My mother's business experience was invaluable to the Drexler wheat business. She attended to the dispatch and invoicing of grain as well as paying the wages for all workers involved in the business and negotiating with growers and agents.

My mother was incredibly accurate with figures. When I was a small boy, in the evening before going to bed my father would tell me a story while my mother would quiz me on arithmetic. That was a short chapter in my life.

In Slovakia there was a class system dependent on education and financial circumstances. In Špačince most of the farmers, wheat and fruit growers were of a lower education standard. Boys and girls left school early and joined their mothers and fathers on the farms and in the wheat fields. My family was considered of a higher class, and the people in the village addressed my mother as 'Milostiva Pani' (graceful lady). It took some time for her to get used to this custom. However, she preferred to ignore the class system and in a very short time she became a friend and confidant of many wives of the farmers and growers. My parents were warmly received by the villagers and were made welcome in their homes. This helped them to maintain the loyalty of the staff at a time when hatred of the Jews was encouraged by the government.

One of the biggest problems for women was the culture of alcohol and violence. Often they were short of money to buy necessities for their children, since the husbands spent the money buying alcohol. My mother would always give the women a small loan of money to help. She never expected to be repaid.

In order to devote more time to the business, my mother employed Maria, a devout Catholic, as a cook and housekeeper for our family. Maria was married to Miklós and they had four children. She was a very loyal employee and she would confide in my mother about her financial problems. Miklós was one of the husbands who spent his money on alcohol and made life unbearable for Maria. On hearing about the problem, my father then employed Miklós to look after our cows and horses on the understanding that his wages were to be handed over to Maria.

Many years later my mother told me that my father was a very hard worker, but because of his generous nature, he never became rich. He, like his father before him, always helped his community before helping himself.

There were about twelve Jewish families in Špačince and the surrounding areas. They were either wheat growers or provided services to the growers and farming community of the district. But the majority of the people living in Špačince were devout Catholics. In their homes they had a crucifix hanging from the wall in most of the rooms. Also, a painting of the Madonna, Mary the Mother of Jesus, would adorn the main room. The elderly widows of the village always wore black and would cross themselves frequently.

They all attended Mass on Sundays. The priest had a tremendous power over his congregation. He often preached that the Jews killed Jesus and thus encouraged anti-Semitism among the population. Sometimes, following his sermons, the young men would throw stones into Jewish homes. I could not understand the connection between church and violence. Their action of throwing stones into Jewish homes, including ours, scared me. But when my father would put his arms around me and tell me not to worry I felt safe. He was my hero.

In summer I would wait outside our front gate for my father to return from the city. I remember one occasion when he was running late – my mother called me to come inside and go to bed, but I refused and ran down to the lower gate instead. My mother came running after me with a large wooden spoon in her hand calling 'Palko, come inside and go to bed'. I continued running in circles, laughing and tripping over, until she caught me.

A lot of fruit was grown in Špačince and much of it was used in cooking. Some of the best fruit dumplings were made with apricots and plums in the middle, and then rolled in breadcrumbs or ground poppy seeds. In the summer months, a common sight in the village were the farmers' daughters taking large pots of freshly made apricot or plum dumplings wrapped in tea towels out to the fields for their fathers' lunch. Some would run with the pot; others would ride a bicycle.

My mother's fruit dumplings were the best. Later, when we moved to Sydney, she continued the tradition of making dumplings in the summer when apricots and plums were in season. She didn't just make dumplings – mouth-watering cakes, including poppy seed and walnut rolls, chocolate kugelhoffs and her famous apple strudel often came out of her kitchen.

I can remember a Mr and Mrs Schwartz – a Jewish couple who had a large farming property situated at the end of Špačince. The Schwartzs did not have children. They were often at our home and were very good friends of my parents.

My father was a very patient and gentle man and the only time I saw him angry was when he had an argument with Mr Schwartz. The Schwartzs were planning to leave Špačince without giving any notice to their employees or anyone else. My father thought this to be a desperate move and opposed their plans. This was in the summer of 1943 when our lives were in much greater danger than my parents realised.

Friday was my favourite day of the week. It was a comforting feeling to see my mother preparing for Shabbat. Although assisted by Maria, my mother was in total control of the meal and only she did all the baking. My mother always began with the kneading of dough for the challahs. I was fascinated by the way she plaited the dough. She always baked at least four challahs, sometimes more, depending on the number of guests we had for Shabbat.

My parents were observant Jews: my father laid tefilin[1] every morning, our family maintained a kosher home and we did not cook on Shabbat. During the winter months my mother prepared a delicacy – the very thick soup known as chollent. It consisted of smoked brisket, broad beans, barley, onion, potato and raw eggs in their shell, all put in a huge earthenware pot on Friday afternoon and placed on a special portable coal stove, where it cooked overnight and was ready for lunch on Saturday. The aroma of Mother's chollent filtered through our home. We ate it with the homemade challah after returning home from synagogue.

In mid 1943 many of the Jewish families in Špačince began to leave Slovakia in search of a safer place to live, as they were frightened what would happened to them under the new regime. As it was very important to ensure that the required ten men were available to pray on Shabbat in our small synagogue, several of the families would invite single Jewish men from Trnava to stay over the weekend. During this time my family invited two men.

Often one of them would be my Uncle Max, my father's youngest brother. At thirty-two years of age Max was still a bachelor. He lived in Trnava and worked for a bank. I loved my Uncle Max. He always brought me sweets and had time to play with me and tell me funny stories. My grandmother Regina also loved Max. I could see by the way she fussed over him. He was very good looking and was the only member of the family who wore glasses.

After March 1944 I never saw Uncle Max again. He was in hospital for a few months; he was suffering from leukaemia and died in June 1944. Our family was heartbroken, especially my grandmother.

Shortly after Max's death, my grandmother went to live with Jozef, her middle son. Known as Josko, he was the manager of a large agricultural estate near Budmerice, about one hour's drive southwest from Špačince. There they grew wheat, barley, corn and fruit. The estate was a safer place for my grandmother to live.

I recall visiting my grandmother at Budmerice with my father. We went by horse and buggy. I always had tremendous fun when we were together. He was a gentle and very patient man who loved his family above all. He also took me to the fields with him as he inspected the progress of the wheat. My father knew everyone by name and it appeared that everyone knew him and greeted him. I have always treasured these memories.

Easter was a very special time in Špačince. As well as going to church there was a carnival atmosphere in Špačince. The young men and women would wear colourful national costumes and dance to the tunes played on a harmonica. The young girls looked especially lovely as they twirled around in their frilly skirts. The speciality of Easter was the handpainted hard-boiled eggs that they gave out to everyone.

I also remember the wheat harvest celebration, when the young men and women dressed up in the Slovak national costumes. The women wore flowers in their hair and sang and danced. I was allowed to sit on one of the saddled horses and ride up and down our property. My mother brought out schnapps and shot glasses. All our employees lined up to have a shot of schnapps, and other villagers followed them. Everyone was happy. That was September 1943 and the last of such occasions that my family celebrated.

As a boy, my most prized possession was a black wooden rocking horse. It had a flowing black mane and tail. I just loved this horse – to me he was real. I would sit on his leather saddle and hold the reins, and rock backwards and forwards for ages, especially during the colder months when it was too cold to be outside. I would imagine that we were riding out in the fields.

I vividly remember one afternoon when I was peacefully rocking on my horse, there was suddenly the shrieking of an air raid siren followed by the roar of aircraft flying low overhead. My mother rushed into the living room, grabbed me off my horse and together we ran from our house down over the creek to a wooded area where we joined with many of our neighbours until all was quiet. I was scared, especially as my father was away on business. This was really the first time I experienced true fear.

In 1942 the Tiso regime confiscated all valuables owned by Jews. Our radios and household items including our silver cutlery, our silver candlesticks and our menorahs were confiscated. When it came to the Jewish festival of Chanukah in 1943, celebrating the victory by the Maccabees, we did not have a Chanukiah (candle holder with nine branches) to hold the candles. So my father took a log of wood and attached the lit candles to it, in a makeshift Chanukiah. For eight nights I watched the candles burn on that log of wood. Still today, when I close my eyes I can see the candles flickering in the dark. My father led the Chanukah, singing 'Ma'oz Tzur' (Rock of Ages). He could keep the tune better than my mother.

In December 1943 the village was covered in snow. Christmas preparations were underway for most people. The women came around to show us their creations – black blood sausages. I never understood what they were and I was not allowed to try them either!

The big attraction in the village was the large snowman that I helped my father to build. A few days after we made it my father and I stood in front of the snowman, watching the hard packed ice turn to glistening beads of water. The snowman was melting, and it made me feel very sad.

Life remained on an even plateau for some months until September 1944 when all the privileges held by the Jews were cancelled. Initially the only difference that I could sense was the atmosphere in our home. My parents talked a lot and appeared stressed. My father travelled much less and we no longer had visitors stay over for Shabbat.

Around this time my other grandmother, Maria Weiss, came to live with us. She was eighty-two years old and spent a lot of time in bed since she found walking very difficult. Grandmother Weiss constantly complained about her aches and pains, and called out regularly from her bed. I remember feeling very sorry for her but I could see the additional family stress, especially on my mother's face. My father would distract me from this by encouraging me to go outside and kick my red ball to him. He always had time for me, and always did his best to shield me from the grave realities of our existence.

My childhood in Špačince was altogether a wonderful one, albeit far too short. At age six, the tragedy that would affect me for life was about to occur. I was blissfully unaware of it, for which I am now grateful.

1 Tefilin are leather boxes containing pieces of parchment on which passages from the Old Testament are inscribed. Leather straps are attached to the boxes. It is a sign of faith and devotion and worn by men during the morning prayers. The box is placed on the forehead and the straps wrapped around the hand and up the arm.

CHAPTER

II

UNDER ARREST

The first dramatic change in our lives that I was aware of was in September 1944, when our business and property were taken over by 'Arizators' – trustees appointed by the government. A fellow by the name of Novak – a well-dressed man from Trnava who wore a similar grey suit to my father – was appointed to take over my father's business. Pán Novak came every day for about a week for long meetings with my father about the change in ownership. Shortly after, Novak, his wife, three children and his mother moved into our house. My parents and I were forced to live in the attached apartment, which was previously occupied by my grandmother Regina. There was no room for my other grandmother, Maria Weiss, to live with us in the small apartment, but fortunately my mother was able to arrange for her to stay with a friendly Christian woman in the village.

The apartment was very small, compared with the main part of our house. It consisted of a living room with a small kitchen at one end, and a bedroom where my parents slept. I slept on a settee in the living room. Everything was different. My parents, more often than ever, talked in German so that I would not understand their conversation. However, I sensed that something was not right, although my father did everything possible to maintain a calm atmosphere. He would sit with me as I did jigsaw puzzles and would now and then put a piece of the puzzle in its correct place which gave me a secure feeling that we were doing the puzzle together. He would read to me and best of all we would kick my big red ball to each other. As he was no longer working he was able to spend more time with me. His warm, calm and caring nature, together with his sense of humour, made him a wonderful father. I worshipped him.

From my memory, the changeover was very civil. I enjoyed playing with the youngest son of the Novak family, who was my age. The older son, aged eight, and the ten year old daughter sometimes joined us when we played hide-and-seek. I doubt they had any more knowledge than me as to what was really happening at the time. We were just children who saw no divide between our religions or ethnicities.

Unbeknown to me, the next few months were extremely dangerous for us because the Nazis were conducting a further roundup of Jewish families. My mother believed that they were looking for adult males, so she would send my father out of the village when they were warned the Nazi patrols were expected in our area. She would prepare a picnic basket for my father and me. We bicycled, and I sat in front of my father as he peddled. It was the summer of 1944. The weather was beautiful. The sun shone every day. My father showed me the different grains growing in the fields. He also pointed out the sunflower seeds and the most interesting of all –

the poppy seeds. He broke off a poppy seedpod so that I could dissect it. It was a lot of fun. It was years later that I found out the real reason for these picnics.

I turned six on 29 June 1944. The year before when I turned five I remember there was a big party with my uncles Josko and Max, my grandmothers and various family friends who travelled from Trnava to celebrate with me. This year there was no birthday celebration.

I began school in September 1944. The school was about ten minutes walk from our home on the other side of the creek. I did not realise at the time, but Jewish children were not allowed to attend school. However, the headmaster, who was also the teacher for my grade, was a good friend of my parents and he turned a blind eye in my case. But my school life in Špačince was short lived – it lasted for only one week.

Just before this, in late August, the Slovak National Uprising had broken out. Led by 20,000 Slovak partisans and aided by 60,000 soldiers of the rebel Czechoslovak Army in Slovakia, the rising attempted to overthrow the Tiso-led Slovak People's Party government, and free Slovakia from its dependence on Nazi Germany. The uprising depended on the Soviet Army invading Slovakia through German lines on two fronts.

The rising was the longed-for opportunity to crush the fascists and establish a government before the Soviets arrived and established a communist puppet regime. At the same time Warsaw had risen. The Germans were in no mood to be merciful – their end objective was the destruction of Slovakia.

The Soviet government regarded the Slovak resistance as politically suspect and did not inform the Slovaks of a change in Soviet strategy. On 29 August 1944, the Germans invaded Slovakia and held supremacy over the rebels. The resistance continued until 27 October 1944 when the Germans took over the headquarters of the rebels in Banska Bystrica, the regional capital which was situated in central Slovakia in a valley where three major mountain ranges intersected. The army retreated to the mountains and continued with guerrilla warfare until Liberation. About ten per cent of the partisans were Jewish.

After crushing the uprising, the Nazis began their final roundup of the remaining Jewish families in Slovakia. I was pulled out of school and my father made arrangements for the three of us to go into hiding with a Christian family on their farm outside Špačince. We hid in the attic where there were two mattresses and a lot of straw. We had to be very quiet so as not be heard by the farm workers. I learnt later from my mother that my father paid the farmer a great deal of money for hiding us and supplying us with food. The price was high but so was the farmer's risk – the penalty for hiding Jews was death.

It was a difficult time. Every day I smelled the baking of homemade sour dough bread coming from the kitchen. It was enticing and made me hungry. I never got to taste it though. My patient father did his best to keep me occupied and calm during these weeks. I remember him reading to me and teaching me to write numbers and letters. Mother, on the other hand, was extremely nervous. She was startled by every sound. We had to speak in whispers as she was afraid that we would be overheard by an employee and be reported to the police.

My father had packed my favourite storybook about Jánošik the Slovak Robin Hood. Juro Jánošik, the leader of the Slovak mountain boys, was a great legendary hero who fought injustice and oppression and was a symbol of justice and of truth. On the cover of the book was a sketch of the hero wearing his mountaineers hat, his rucksack on his back and holding a staff in his right hand. I would listen to my father for hours, reading the stories of my favourite hero over and over again.

I did not realise it then, but these weeks spent in the farmer's attic was when I lost my childhood.

It was probably early November 1944 when we were forced to go back to the apartment because the farmer became very nervous with the increase of German soldiers in the area. We were only back in the apartment for two days before my father made arrangements for us to go into hiding again. However, Mother and I were separated from him – she and I hid with one farming family and my father hid with another. After only two weeks my mother and I were forced to return to the apartment as this farmer, too, became scared when he heard our names being broadcast on the local radio and warning that the penalty for hiding Jews was death. Understandably, his own safety was more important to him than any money we could pay.

My father stayed hidden and did not know that we

had been evicted from the farmer's property. My mother was even more nervous not being able to contact him to let him know we were back in the apartment.

Mother knew a man in Trnava who had several motor vehicles and was involved in smuggling Jews out of the area. I remember very clearly leaving the apartment in the frosty early hours, sometime after midnight one night, to walk to Trnava with my mother to contact this man. We were dressed in heavy overcoats with hoods for the cold. It was dangerous to walk on the main road so we went through wheat fields instead. We could hear the piercing sounds of the Germans driving on the main road in their trucks and motorbikes with sidecars. It was very frightening.

I became very tired during the seven kilometre walk from Špačince to Trnava. There were various haystacks in the fields so my mother suggested I lean against one and have a sleep. I don't know how long I slept for, but when I woke up I got a terrible shock – I couldn't see my mother anywhere. I was terrified. I quickly walked around the haystack and to my great relief found her on the other side, keeping an eye out for Nazis on the road. From here we could see a convoy of military trucks.

We were successful in avoiding the Nazis and eventually arrived in Trnava at daybreak. We made our way to the home of the man who supposedly smuggled the Jews out of the area. The journey was for nothing – he could not help us. Mother was distraught. The area was now fully occupied by the Germans – we were surrounded.

We walked towards a church. Mother knocked at

the side door and was greeted by a clergyman. He let us in and my mother did a lot of talking and he asked a lot of questions. She gave him money and he gave her what looked like official papers. Later my mother told me that he was a Protestant pastor. He supplied us with the papers to certify that we had been baptised and were now members of the Protestant Church. She was desperate for our safety.

I cannot remember how we returned to our home in Špačince, but I know we did not walk.

The Nazis were everywhere in Špačince, billeted in bigger homes. This my mother found out in the most frightening way. Late one night she left the apartment, crossing the courtyard to use the toilet. To her surprise, a tall man in a black SS uniform came out of the toilet and on seeing my mother, who froze at the sight of him, asked in German: 'Jüdin?' (Jewess) All she could say was 'yes' and at the same time, she wet her pants. The Nazi shouted: 'By the time I've finished with you, you'll more than wet yourself', and he stormed off back into the main house.

Many years later my mother told me that on that night, after meeting that man, she became so desperate, not being able to communicate with my father and not knowing where he was, that in her panic she decided to take her own life. She swallowed a bottle of aspirin. When she suddenly remembered that I was asleep in the other room further panic went through her mind. Hurriedly, she got warm milk and drank it in order to vomit up the aspirin.

The following night my father was also forced out of his hiding place because of the penalties announced over the radio. He returned to the apartment, finding my mother and me there. Having the three of us together again made my mother feel better, but now we were trapped in the apartment, and my parents were constantly talking together in German. They did their best to prepare me for the events that were to follow. They patiently explained that we would soon have to leave the apartment and would be taken by policemen to a big place where there would be a lot of Jews, but assured me that we would all be together.

It happened the next night – a loud knock on the front door. My mother quickly told my father to hide in the wardrobe as she thought that perhaps it was only my father they were after, not women and children. She opened the door and was confronted by two Gestapo men, very tall and broad, and two members of the local police. I got such a shock at seeing these four men at the door that no prior preparation could ever prevent my reaction. I vomited.

The men asked for my father. Rather than risk the safety of Mother and me, Father came out of the wardrobe. The two Gestapo men announced that they we were now under arrest and that should pack two small bags. One of the policemen went to fetch our coach driver, Miklós, who was ordered to get the horses and coach ready for our transport. Miklós was wearing a baggy, well-worn three-piece suit, while my father was wearing an elegant tailor-made three-piece suit. One of the Gestapo men ordered Miklós to give his clothes to Father and for Father to give his suit to Miklós. Miklós was extremely distressed with this order. My father calmly took Miklós by the arm and told him that it was all right to do as they'd been ordered. They quietly changed clothes.

My mother packed two small cases with our clothing. In addition she took two of my small blankets, which she attached to the outside of one of the cases. One of these blankets has remained in my possession to this day.

My grandmother Maria suddenly appeared at the door of the apartment and was also arrested. I remember she was shouting loudly in protest, while my parents remained calm.

We were ordered to get into the coach. I was very frightened. Miklós, uncomfortable in my father's suit, was ordered to get up front take us to the local police station.

When we arrived there my grandmother and I were ordered to sit in one room while my parents were pushed into an adjoining room. I heard a lot of shouting at my parents and then a kind of lashing sound. I did not understand the situation. I was very frightened. My grandmother tried to calm me by stroking my head and shoulders.

Later I found out that my mother and father were stripped to the waist, and then whipped on the back by a policeman with a horsewhip. The police wanted to know where my parents had hidden their valuables. Did they hide them with Shulko, our neighbour and friend? They denied this. I was on the verge of crying when my parents came out of the room. They appeared to be exceptionally calm after this harrowing experience. My mother could see how upset I was and held me very close to her. My father supported my mother.

We were ordered back to the coach and were taken by Miklós from Špačince to a police station in Trnava. The two Gestapo men drove ahead in their car. On arrival at Trnava police station the four of us were pushed into a cell, where we were locked up for the remainder of the night. My mother made me comfortable on the only bed in the cell, wrapping the two blankets she had brought around me to keep me warm. I was completely exhausted and slept until morning.

In the morning we were given some coffee and bread. The Gestapo then took us to the railway station. At the station were other families looking as forlorn as we were. They were also clutching small cases. We stood there for a long time. Eventually a passenger train arrived and everyone was ordered aboard. I sat between my parents who made conversation with the people on the seat opposite. My grandmother, who sat next to us, was silent.

After a short time the train stopped at Sered railway station where guards, all dressed in green uniforms, shouted: 'everyone off the train'. We did as we were told. I could feel my body trembling as I looked at the scowled look on the guards' faces; I was frightened even though I had the comfort of my father's hand holding mine. The vicious guards formed a barrier around us as they herded us into the grounds of Sered Labour Camp.

We went with many other families into a large room that had double bunks in lines throughout the room and a few tables and benches in the centre. I looked around the room at the other frightened people as my father led me to one of the lower bunks. It was cold, but I was somewhat warmed up by the cup of warm soup and slice of brown bread that my mother lined up to get for me.

People began to change into their nightwear. I got such a shock when my parents took off their shirts and I saw their backs, which were black and blue from the beatings that they had endured the night before in the police station in Špačince. Other people around asked them what had happened.

My parents got into one bunk together. I was in a bunk opposite them and my grandmother slept in a bunk in front of me. As I lay there, drifting off, I remember thinking that it must be uncomfortable sleeping together in one bunk. And then I fell asleep.

LIFE IN SERED

The town of Sered is situated sixty kilometres northwest of Slovakia's capital Bratislava. The camp my family was taken to, near Sered, was converted from a military camp into a forced labour camp for Jews in 1942. Before the renovations and additions were complete, the camp had become a collection centre for Jewish mass deportation to Poland. Hlinka guards guarded the camp.

After the last transport to Poland on the Day of Atonement (the most sacred Holy day in the Jewish religion) in 1942, the 1300 remaining prisoners in the camp were involved in the manufacture of furniture and were treated reasonably well. In August 1944, during the Slovak national uprising, the camp gates were opened and many of the young people left for central Slovakia to join the rebel forces.

The camp became operational again after the Germans occupied western Slovakia in late August 1944. One of Eichmann's main henchmen, Alois Brunner, known for his cruelty and hatred for the Jews, was appointed as the commandant.

The first thing I remember of the early days in Sered was my parents and the other adults leaving for work each morning, and only returning when it was dark. My mother and father both worked in a furniture workshop near the camp. It was winter and extremely cold. Children and the elderly remained in the dormitory throughout the day. I anxiously awaited my parents' return each evening. My father would sit with me on my bunk and tell me stories, including my favourite, about the great Slovak hero, Jánošik. Although always outnumbered, Jánošik won over his enemies and saved the Slovak people. I wonder now if my father was trying to tell me that Jánošik would save us.

When I was older I often thought about those precious moments with my father. I always wondered if he was trying to make me understand that good would always triumph over evil.

While my father sat with me, Mother would stand in line holding our metal bowls to get our evening rations. I remember sitting between my parents at a small table in the dormitory while we ate. My grandmother sat opposite.

We weren't at the camp for very long before my mother and I were separated from my father and my grandmother. My mother and I were sent to a smaller dormitory for women and children on the first floor of a large building. My father was sent with the men to another area of the camp. My grandmother was taken to a dormitory for elderly women.

During the daytime while my mother was away at work, there were organised informal classes for the children, where stories were read and songs were sung. Despite having the company of playmates, I was not happy. My life had been turned upside down. I longed for the comfort of our home in Špačince. I wanted to ride my wooden horse in our living room near the open fire. I missed playing with my father.

The daily food, although nothing like my mother's cooking, was reasonable. Two men brought the evening meal of soup and bread to the women's dormitory each night. One man pushed the trolley along the corridor while the other ladled the soup out and gave out the bread.

One evening I got such a surprise seeing my father pushing the trolley along the corridor towards our dormitory. I had not seen him for about three weeks. He was wearing different clothes from those he had arrived in – he was now dressed in grey pants, jacket and cap. I remember him putting his arms around me and giving me a big hug and kisses. It was a wonderful moment, though I had never seen such sadness in his brown eyes before. That cold night in December 1944 was the last time I saw my father.

TRANSPORT TO AUSCHWITZ

During my research I found a record of the departure date of our transport from Sered. It was on 19 December 1944 (two days after seeing my father with the food trolley) that mother and I were assembled outside in the cold with all the other women and children and our small suitcases containing our meagre belongings. I noticed immediately how very strained my mother looked. She said to me, 'Palko, hold on to my hand, and do not let go, whatever happens.' We were then herded like cattle onto the trains. My mother held my hand so tightly that she was hurting me, but she was determined that we would not be separated. Guards were shouting 'Schnell! Schnell!' (quick, quick). Children were crying; mothers tried to comfort them. There was more shouting and pushing by the guards. Once the cattle carriage that my mother and I were pushed into was full, the doors were closed and bolted. There was nowhere to sit except the floor, and not everyone could sit down at the same time because we were so tightly packed in. There were no windows, and the only light came from the cracks in the sliding doors. The only object in the carriage was a bucket in one corner to be used as a toilet.

'Where is Tatichko?'[1] I cried, desperate for my father. 'We cannot leave without Tatichko'. 'He will come later with the other men,' my mother assured me.

It was very cold. My mother put one of her small blankets on the floor for me to sit on, and wrapped the other one around me. We were crammed in like sardines in a tin. When she could, my mother would sit close to me. I was frozen in thought and feeling. I was hungry. No one knew where we were going. Everyone was frightened. The train eventually began its journey, but to where? The women talked with each other, perhaps to console themselves. I remember a little girl screaming out 'I am cold, I am hungry'. This was the strangest journey of my life – nothing can ever compare. I lapsed into a kind of sleep, dreaming that I was back home in Špačince playing ten pins with my father.

The train journey seemed to last forever. There was a lot of stopping and starting of the train because of damaged railway lines. Detours had to be taken. The train stopped at various stations, where the doors were opened and soup was ladled into our small metal dishes from a big pot on the platform. Bread was also distributed. We were not allowed to leave the carriage. At the stations the toilet bucket was emptied. The stench from the bucket within the carriage was unbearable.

As the anxiety grew among the women I became quite terrified. From time to time one of the women would let out a piercing scream, while others cried uncontrollably. My mother was remarkably calm, and helped the women around her to settle down. She told them very calmly that it could not be much further and that they would then be reunited with their husbands. Her calmness was a great help to me. However, thinking back now, I do not know how she was able to appear so controlled on the surface. My mother was just like all the other women in the cattle carriage – she did not have the answers. But she did have faith in the Almighty.

At one of the stops we seemed to wait for a long time. No-one knew why we had stopped for so long. Unbeknown to us, our transport had arrived in Auschwitz.

Auschwitz was in turmoil. The Red Army was advancing through southern Poland towards Krakow. All evidence of the death factory had to be obliterated. The gas chambers and crematoriums had been destroyed and evacuation of those still living had to be organised.

Our transport of frightened women and children stood on the siding at Auschwitz. The concentration camp was shutting down and did not want the burden of more Jews. Eventually the train began moving and we were sent west to a place I later came to know as Theresienstadt.

How different the outcome for me would have been if we had arrived in Auschwitz when the gas chambers and crematoriums were still in operation. I believe it was my mother's faith and an amazing stroke of luck that the two of us survived.

OUR LIFE IN
THERESIENSTADT

If Auschwitz was the Kingdom of death;
Terezín was the Kingdom of deceit.

Chaim Potok

On 23 December 1944, after travelling for five days
we arrived at Theresienstadt. It was very overcast
and bitterly cold. We were herded off the cattle train
and taken to an area where we waited in line to be
registered. I remember I had a terrible need to go to the
toilet as I could not go on the train. My mother took me
by the hand away from the people to an area, which was
like a hole with a railing. I relieved myself but could
not comprehend that the void was filled with dried
excrement. I'd never seen anything like it.

We returned to the line of people and eventually my
mother completed our registration. I was identified as
number 42 of Transport XXVI/1. This identification
appeared on my registration card, health immunisation
card and ration card in Theresienstadt and this was
how I was known. All the mothers and their sons were
ordered to follow a man, who was wearing a shabby
grey suit, to the Boys' Home at 17 Hauptstrasse, where
our mothers were instructed to leave us. This was the
first time in my life I had ever been separated from
my mother. I was six years old. I had been in a cattle
car for five days, huddled on the floor in the cold, and
now I was to be on my own without my mother. I was

in a daze; I understood nothing of what was going on around me.

I felt so lost and so alone in this huge building – the walls seemed to reach the sky, except instead of sky there was a roof. The staff at the Boys' Home were Czech women who were very kind and tried to pacify the younger boys like myself, but all I could think was that I would soon wake up from this nightmare.

The Boys' Home consisted of a large dormitory with double bunks, a dining area and a school area. It was very strange. It was empty when we arrived. My mother later found out and told me that the reason the home was empty was that the boys had been transported to Auschwitz two months earlier.

My mother was housed in a large dormitory in the Hamburg Barracks in Bahnhofstrasse 3, which was at the other end of Theresienstadt. Shortly after our arrival my mother found out that her mother Maria, who was on the same transport as us, was housed in the aged people's dormitories.

Theresienstadt ('Terezín' in Czech), a fortified town sixty kilometres northwest of Prague, was built in 1780 by Emperor Joseph II as a garrison town and named in honour of his mother, Maria Theresa. The fortress town, systematically planned with barracks and surrounded by walls and a moat, was perfect for a ghetto. In late 1941 it became the holding centre for the Jews from the Czech lands as well as for elderly German Jews. German Jews had to pay for their place, being told they would be relocated to a spa town where they would have pleasant accommodation. On arrival they quickly learnt that in fact the camp was the waiting room for further deportations to the East.

The food was terrible. I was unable to eat it. The daily soup was powdery and the artificial taste made me vomit every time. All I could eat was a little potato and some bread.

I remember spending the days in the classroom in the Boys' Home where we were read stories, taught songs and did some drawings. Erev Shabbat was very special in the Boys' Home. Shabbat dinner consisted of sardine open sandwiches, which were placed in the middle of the tables. We each had a little plate in front of us. I remember the older boys taking one sandwich onto their little plate and putting another one just in front of their plates 'to have a reserve'. All of this was so foreign to me. I had never eaten sardines before. They looked awful and tasted even worse. I just could not eat them.

Friday nights were special again because mothers were allowed to come and see their children. I waited each week for Friday night to come, as I was desperate to see my mother and feel her arms around me. I did not know where we were or why we were there, and worst of all, where my father was. Mother said on the horrible journey to Theresienstadt that Tatichko would come later. Each Friday night I hoped that this would be the day my parents would come and see me together.

The women in Theresienstadt did not have to work on Saturdays. It was the only day of rest in Theresienstadt. If it was not snowing on Saturdays, my mother came to the Boys' Home to take me out for a walk. She showed me where she lived in the Hamburg Barracks. I had never seen anything like these barracks. There was a main gate that led to a courtyard, which had three-storey buildings on all four sides. I felt closed in by the height around me. My comfort came from holding my mother's hand; that gave me a little security. One Saturday morning when it was snowing my mother did not come. I was so desperate to see her that I pestered the lady in charge to let me go to her. Eventually, she agreed and dressed me in warmer clothes that were far too big for me. She gave me boots that were also too big for me but that enabled me to walk in the snow. I walked in the bitter cold, desperately hoping that I was headed in the right direction. Why was I in this strange place? It then began to snow again and my thoughts turned to my father. Where was he? I wished we could build a snowman together.

I still do not know how I found my way to the Hamburg Barracks in the snow on my own. When I arrived at my mother's dormitory I was shivering and could not control my lips. Mother was surprised to see me and put her arms around me, which made me feel so much better. I had missed the warmth and softness of her embrace. I remember her giving me some of her bread. We talked for a little while and then we walked back together to the Boys' Home. I felt calmer having spent time with her.

The weather in January 1945 in Theresienstadt was freezing and the sky was always grey. I got sick because of the cold. There was never enough heating in the Boys' Home and I could not eat the food. I developed a nasty cough and cold which did not improve as the weeks went on. Each Friday night when she saw me, my mother became more and more worried. I was also losing weight. She approached the authorities in Theresienstadt and appealed to them to allow me to live with her in the Hamburg Barracks. Her persistence paid off as her request was eventually granted. This encouraged other mothers to do the same and have the younger children live with them. The people looking after the children in the home were happy to let our mothers take responsibility for us.

Mother and I moved into a smaller dormitory, which had eight bunks in Room 122 on the first floor of the Hamburg Barracks. We each had a bunk to sleep in – she slept on the top bunk and I on the bottom.

To get our food we had to take our tin bowls and walk to another area, line up, show our ration cards and were then issued with soup and a small serving of a potato in gravy. Occasionally we also received a piece of meat. My mother and I would walk back to the barracks where we ate our meal together. I do not remember how the bread was rationed; it may have been given out every few days as my mother always had some saved bread in the dormitory for when I got hungry.

My mother told me that after about two months in Theresienstadt she and some other women thought they were pregnant as they ceased to menstruate. However, they were quickly told by some of the longer serving female inmates that there was something put in the food to stop them menstruating.

Several years later when my mother told me this she was still convinced there was something put in the food. Historians who claim that the cause of the women not menstruating was due to extreme trauma and malnutrition have refuted this story.

While I lived in the Boys' Home, the days were structured. However when I lived with my mother in the dormitory, my days were different. I remember my mother making sure I had something to eat before she had to report to the line up area with other women. From there they marched to the farm where they spent each day working as farm labourers.

Most of the work in the ghetto was concerned with maintenance. The production of haberdashery, cardboard and other goods was undertaken for 'outside' enterprises. Women worked on mica splitting (for use as insulation materials in electrical appliances) for the Wehrmacht.

Work was compulsory for prisoners between sixteen and sixty years of age, but in reality even younger and older people had to work. Prisoners did not try to avoid the labour. Sometimes they gained small favours, and also the food rations for workers were slightly higher. On the other hand, wages paid in ghetto money – issued in May 1943 – were a mere formality and served the sole purpose of painting an even more deceitful picture of Theresienstadt.

Shops had been opened in Theresienstadt as early as 1942. One could use vouchers to buy certain types of products that had been confiscated upon arrival at the ghetto. Later a café was opened too, where prisoners who were able to obtain tickets could sit drinking Ersatz Kaffe for two hours and listen to swing, or light classical music. In May 1943 the Bank established by the Jewish self-administration began operations, issuing bank notes, without any real value, as a substitution for vouchers. A picture of Moses bearing the Ten Commandments was on the notes.

The only value the currency had was to buy limited items of dubious value from the shops. Good clothing, shoes, feather quilts, even brushes and combs were taken for the use of Germans. Items of lesser quality, down to half-squeezed tubes of toothpaste, notebooks and boxes of matches went to the ghetto's own warehouse, to be sent later to the ghetto 'stores', where they could be purchased back by the prisoners.

Every day Mother would beg or steal an egg and/or a potato from the farm and smuggle them into the camp at great risk. She told me that the guards would beat any woman caught with food.

In the dormitory there was a pot-belly stove where my mother would fry the potatoes and eggs for me. This was a delicacy compared to the slop we were served at Theresienstadt. I was always hungry but if it were not for my mother, I would not have survived. I would have been just another of the many children who died of hunger and disease.

I sometimes went to classes in Theresienstadt while my mother worked at the farm. The classes were held in other barracks, but they were sporadic. I have no idea what I learnt, but I do remember singing, listening to stories and doing some pencil sketches. The teachers were friendly and seemed concerned about me, as I was often unwell. I played with other children from different parts of Czechoslovakia. I remember playing in the street – we played hide and seek and other imaginative games that did not require toys, as we did not have any. I also remember the curfew that prohibited us from leaving the barracks at night. Throughout each long day that my mother was away working I looked forward to her return – I was always scared that she might not. I lived in an atmosphere of fear.

Once a week all the women and children of the Hamburg Barracks would assemble in the courtyard with towels in their hands and we would be marched, under supervision, to the communal shower block. As children we made a game of imitating the common ritual. We took turns in supervising a group of boys and girls as far as the shower block and back again.

We had to line up with our ration cards for all of our meals. Breakfast consisted of some kind of a coffee substitute. Although I was always hungry, lunch was an awful tasting soup, which I dreaded. It was made from dried ground lentils or potato and turnip. Sometimes dinner was soup again and some gravy with an occasional piece of meat and a small potato. A small ration of bread was also distributed daily to each prisoner.

I don't remember seeing many German guards around Theresienstadt; mostly they were Czech. A special unit of the Protectorate gendarmerie was also active in Theresienstadt, serving as guards and escort officers. There were Nazi collaborators among them – especially among the commanding officers; they too tortured Jews. I remember a very strict German Jewish woman in charge of the Hamburg Barracks where my mother and I lived, and how afraid my mother was of her. Her name was Frau Grimwald. Frau Grimwald and her assistant Frau Schey were fanatical about the cleanliness of the stairway and the toilet. After people used the toilet one of them would rush in to check if it was left clean.

There were some lighter moments in the camp. The children and women would imitate the guards. Mother wrote a poem about these female guards and their passion for the sole toilet in our block. The poem written in pencil was passed around from woman to woman and they all laughed until they had tears in their eyes. I had not heard such laughter since leaving home. This was a welcome diversion in between the many sad and tragic moments in the camp.

I dreaded the communal toilets and showers in Theresienstadt. The toilets had an overpowering smell of chlorine, which made me sick to my stomach. Even to this day I hate the smell of chlorine. There was only one toilet in the three levels of the Hamburg Barracks and I hated to use it because of the strict inspection by the German women. Luckily I managed to find some single toilets in another building.

The winter in Theresienstadt was freezing and therefore most of the children were restricted to staying inside. As soon as the cold lessened we played in the streets while our mothers worked. As children we were allowed to roam around the streets and explore. What I hated most was the stench in the streets from foul foods and excrement as well as the stench from the dead bodies that were loaded onto carts and taken for burial. It was enough to make anyone sick.

One night I remember I woke up feeling as if my chest was being pulled. I screamed and my mother quickly jumped out of her bunk and took my top off to find that I was covered in worms. The worms were coming from the timber frame of the bed. My mother quickly cleaned the worms from my body. She boiled some water on the pot-belly stove and then thoroughly wiped the timber frames of our bunks. As I had woken the other women in the dormitory with my screaming they saw that their beds were also worm-ridden. Everyone had to clean their bunk frames that night.

I also remember when lice raged in the Hamburg Barracks. My hair was full of it; I kept scratching my head, which made it worse. The smell of lice in the barracks was horrible. My mother tried so hard to get rid of it. She boiled water on the pot-belly stove and sterilised an old comb that she'd found, then she ran the comb through my head to get rid of the lice. I remember her doing it morning and night for several days. She eventually got them all out; she was so patient.

In our small dormitory with only eight double bunks, there were three other younger children. One of the children was a four year old dark-haired girl, Eva. Her mother, Magda Steiner, looked after her. They also came from Slovakia. Because of the circumstances, my mother and Magda Steiner became good friends and supported each other. At the end of war Eva's father did not return and she and her mother migrated first to Israel and then in 1956, to Australia.

My mother and Magda Steiner resumed their friendship in Sydney and were still of tremendous support to each other for many years after that. They would spend many hours on the phone reliving the past and worrying about their children.

However, Eva's and my paths only crossed in recent years due to a mutual friend, Helen Doctors, bringing us together. Since then we have seen each other several times, and our meetings are always very special. Eva is the only child survivor from the Hamburg Barracks in Theresienstadt whom I remember and therefore we have tremendous empathy for each other.

My mother was eventually given a better job in the laundry shop. This was where everyone would leave his or her laundry to be washed. My mother had a very sympathetic Dutch Jewish 'boss', Dr Van der Poorten. He organised extra ration cards for me. The ration cards were issued by the Jewish Elders of Theresienstadt, as were the health cards and typhus vaccination cards. One of the coupons entitled me to obtain one quarter of a litre of skimmed milk each day.

In mid-January 1945 the Nazis decided that Jews of mixed Jewish-German marriages from Germany, Austria and the Protectorate were to be sent to Theresienstadt. They filled the vacancies caused by the transports to Auschwitz. In March 1945, 1150 Hungarian Jews, who were originally working on construction of the fortifications around Vienna, followed. Theresienstadt's numbers were rising.

The approaching end of the war and the ever more inevitable defeat of Hitler's Germany made the SS anxious. Despite this, they were still preparing to use Theresienstadt for propaganda once again – as a false alibi hiding the truth of the murder of the Jews. At the same time, however, steps were being taken for the liquidation of all prisoners before the arrival of the Allied armies.

During my research I learnt that Himmler wanted to exploit the Jews as Germany's most valuable capital in negotiations with the Allies. After his negotiation with the former head of the Swiss election chamber, Jean-Marie Musy, a transport was sent to Switzerland from Theresienstadt. For the 1200 people who left on 5 February 1945 it had been an unexpected and happy liberation.

In March 1945 my paternal grandmother, Regina Drexler, who had been in hiding before being taken to the Sered transit camp, arrived in Theresienstadt. She lived in a different building from us. My mother's bedridden mother, Maria Weiss, was in the home for aged prisoners in Room 10–12, a hospital on Langenstrasse 11. Regina brought news that her younger daughter Rezi had been separated from her and taken away, and she did not know where she was. Fortunately her son Josko (my uncle) was still being hidden by a friendly Christian family.

I continued to go to school, play with the other children and, once my grandmothers were also in Theresienstadt, I was able to visit them and spend time there. This helped to fill in the days while my mother was working.

My mother and I had no information from the outside world. It was very frightening and all we could do was to take each day at a time, as we never knew what would happen next. I remember watching the transports come. There were sometimes two or three a week. I would watch anxiously as I was always hoping that my father would arrive on one of the transports. He never did.

My two blankets that my mother hastily took with her when we were arrested in Špačince proved to be of great comfort to me while I was interned in Theresienstadt. We were issued with very coarse thin blankets but the feel of the soft wool of my own blankets next to my skin to keep me warm and the familiar fragrance gave me a sense of security. When I felt hungry and lonely for my father and the home life we had in Špačince, I played a game of make-believe with the figures on the frieze of the blankets. There was a man leading a camel, the pyramid and the palm tree, which was repeated again and again. I transformed myself to another time and another place.

One day Mother and I received a Red Cross parcel that was addressed to another Drexler family but, since that family could not be found, we were the lucky recipients. This parcel contained two small cans of Nestlé sweetened condensed milk, cocoa, two bars of Nestlé chocolate, tea, cigarettes and tinned meat, which we shared with some of the others in the dormitory. To me this parcel was a dream come true, a special treat and an event that I have never forgotten. An elderly man from the Netherlands, who lived downstairs in the Hamburg Barracks, received a parcel but he only wanted the tea, cigarettes and meat, so he gave the rest to my mother for us. We were lucky twice.

In March 1945 Mother heard that Matzah[2] was to be baked during the night. She volunteered to work in the factory at night in order to be able to bring back some of the dough to cook in the frying pan in our dormitory. She hid the dough by flattening it against her breasts. I thought it was bizarre that the guards allowed Matzah to be baked. Later in my life, I questioned my memories of this. Dr Blodig, Director of Terezín Ghetto Museum, confirmed to me in May 2004 that Matzah was indeed made and served in our concentration camp. However I do not remember actually eating Matzah in Theresienstadt.

A curious sight in Theresienstadt were several empty shops. Some had naked mannequins in the window. It was a few years after the war that my mother explained to me the use of the shops in the June 1944 International Red Cross deception.

On 6 April 1945 Eichmann allowed a second visit by the Red Cross, to inspect the ghetto. A beautification was carried out prior to the inspection. An entourage of SS accompanied Dr Lehner and Dr Dunant from the International Red Cross on the tour. The delegation was shown the propaganda film[3] and watched the children perform Hans Krasa's 'Brundibar'. The children's opera was performed 55 times in the ghetto.

Dr Lehner wrote an ecstatic report about Theresienstadt and the SS deception continued. The skilled deceivers were able to pull off the fraud with the 'model ghetto' once again, but the swift progress of events at the end of the war did not allow German propaganda to gain much benefit from it.

The war was slowly drawing to an end, but the suffering of the prisoners was to continue. My only recollection of the Red Cross visit was that suddenly there was a large number of Nazis in uniform in the streets of the ghetto. We, the children, were not allowed to leave the Hamburg Barracks.

One day there was a lot of commotion in the street so I hurried together with the other children to investigate. It was an extraordinary sight in the ghetto. Rows of white buses were parked in the street. I later found out this was 15 April 1945, when the Danish–Jewish prisoners were released and transported back to Denmark in buses hired by the Swedish Red Cross.

From 20 April 1945 onwards a massive influx of Jewish concentration camp prisoners flooded Theresienstadt in the infamous Death Marches. These people, transported from Buchenwald and Gross-Rosen camps, were barely recognisable as human beings – just skeletons covered in skin, some clinging to life, others lying dead in the cattle trucks.

Some of the women in the Hamburg Barracks could not stop crying. They wondered if they would ever see their husbands and relatives again. The women anxiously looked at the men coming out and began searching through the cattle trucks to see if their husbands were among the dead. My mother must have felt unbearable torment. However, she stayed calm, was very much in control, and did not share her inner anxiety with me.

The situation became even worse when it was rumoured that a gas chamber was being built in Theresienstadt. This proved to be true. However, the Nazis left it too late and the gas chamber was never put into operation.

The Hamburg Barracks stood where the railway line ended and all the transports disembarked outside the building. One night I saw for myself the results of Nazi brutality. As a young boy, barely seven years old, I was catapulted into maturity instantaneously. Looking out of the dormitory window that night I saw a group of men coming off a train looking like skin and bones and being half-mad with hunger and exhaustion, wearing remnants of the blue and white striped uniform. They had come from another camp. I was mesmerised by the look of despair in their eyes. I watched them diving into the puddles of water on the ground (it had been raining all that day) and drinking from the puddles because they had had nothing to drink for days. I remember my mother and other women collecting bread and throwing it out to the starving men. The guard called out to the women to stop throwing the bread. I was very scared as I thought the next thing would be that my mother would be taken away and I would be left alone. But nothing further happened.

To the 17,500 prisoners who lived in the ghetto before the arrival of the evacuation transports, 15,000 more people were gradually added. They brought to Theresienstadt various infectious diseases that were very frequent in evacuation transports – especially typhoid fever. Towards the end of the war, and in the first days and weeks after liberation, typhoid fever was to take a terrible toll among the prisoners.

After the first evacuation transports arrived, effective quarantine measures that would isolate the sick from the healthy were next to impossible to implement. The prisoners, exhausted by their hardships, for the most part did not even realise the danger of infection. The first case of typhoid fever was registered on 24 April and after that the infection spread like wild fire. It did not spare prisoners who had lived in Theresienstadt before the arrival of the evacuation transports.

On 2 May 1945 a representative of the International Red Cross, Paul Dunant, arrived in Theresienstadt and took under his protection both the former ghetto and the nearby Gestapo prison in the Small Fortress. The power of the SS in the camp quickly deteriorated – those who until now had ruled the lives of the prisoners were fleeing the town. That did not, however, bring complete freedom to the prisoners, as retreating Wehrmacht and SS units surrounded the camp. Their members, maddened by the inevitable defeat, often fired shots at the prisoners – this too, took its toll at the very end of the war. Not until 8 May did the first divisions of the Red Army pass through Theresienstadt as they made their way to Prague. On 4 May a group of Czech doctors and nurses arrived in Theresienstadt, members of Czech Action for Help. Their help was much needed; especially as prisoners sick with typhoid fever were moved to the ghetto from the Small Fortress. Shortly afterwards members of the Soviet Army medical service also came to assist. However, the main burden of the struggle with the epidemic was still borne by Jewish doctors and nurses. The coordination of all measures taken was assigned to the epidemiologist, Dr Aaron Vedder from the Netherlands.

One morning when I woke up all I could hear was people shouting. 'They have gone, all the guards have gone!' Overnight, all the German and Czech guards had disappeared. This was 8 May 1945, the day the Soviet Army came and liberated Theresienstadt.

I remember Mother and I getting dressed quickly and rushing out of the Hamburg Barracks, joining the crowds running towards the open gates of the ghetto.

My mother clung to me, holding me tightly. The tears welled in her eyes. 'We will be going home, Palko' she called out. She was so excited; I had never seen her like this before. Her excitement made me even more excited.

The soldiers waved and called out greetings. It was a beautiful sunny day and everyone was shouting and cheering. In fact I think it was the first sunny day since we arrived in Theresienstadt. For the first time I saw some of the inmates laugh. Some laughed so much that tears ran down their faces. 'The war is over' the women cried. It was euphoria. Most of the trucks passed the ghetto, but some stayed. I watched all of this from outside the gates where I had never been before.

There were 17,200 survivors in the ghetto at liberation. Of the 15,000 evacuees who returned from camps in the East, 2900 survived. The rest died from typhoid.

We could not go home immediately as transport coordination had to be set up. I thought being liberated meant that Mother and I would meet up with my father and the rest of my family and we would all return to Špačince. I could not wait to see my father again.

The Soviet soldiers brought a lot of tinned meat and other endless supplies that had a totally different taste from anything I had ever eaten before. I remember everyone seeming to be more relaxed but the women were still worried about the gas chambers in Auschwitz. My mother became very concerned about the rest of our family. While we were waiting to go home from Theresienstadt, my mother learnt that there had been many transports from the ghetto to Auschwitz; the last one was on 28 October 1944. These prisoners were the last to die in the gas chambers. Following this the gas chambers of Auschwitz were disbanded.

The typhoid epidemic peaked between 6 and 16 May. Given the risk of infection spreading further, Theresienstadt was closed and a fourteen-day quarantine was proclaimed.

The sick were isolated in hastily established infection wards, but they were not getting appropriate care, medication or nutrition.

In the Hamburg Barracks they had evacuated the typhoid fever infected inmates and transferred them to isolation wards in a hospital building. They closed down the infected dormitories and erected big signs reading; ACHTUNG TYPHUS.[4] Due to this, the number of people becoming ill lessened, and by the end of May it was possible to commence repatriation. The medical authorities that took charge of the camp made sure that the typhus epidemic was over before health clearances were given to the people.

Repatriation was carried on for almost three months. Czechoslovakian citizens were the first to leave Theresienstadt, with others following. The largest groups of prisoners from other countries – especially Hungary and Poland – left in the latter half of June. Many Polish, German and Austrian Jews, however, refused to return to their home countries and asked instead for permission to emigrate to North America or Palestine. They did not leave Theresienstadt until July and August 1945.

Among the repatriated there were children – most of them orphans. They were taken into the care of an organisation led by the great humanist Premysl Pitter. The children were placed in sanitoriums, and later sent to orphanages.

Justice did not prevail for the perpetrators of the crimes. Most of the SS who were active in Theresienstadt managed to escape responsibility for their crimes. Only a fraction of them were caught and tried by the popular tribunal in Litomerice or by courts abroad.

The first Commandant of the camp, Siegfried Seidl, was caught and sentenced to death in Austria. His successor, Anton Burger, escaped from prison twice and died unpunished in the 1990s. The Litomerice tribunal sentenced the third and last Commandant of the camp, Karl Rahm, to death.

We were allowed to leave the 'Town of Deception and Death' on 26 May 1945.[5] On our last day, Mother packed our few belongings. She made sure that both my grandmothers were on the train with us leaving Theresienstadt. Her mother was in the hospital carriage of the train, as she was bedridden. We went back a different way from which we had come. This train had seats on both sides of the carriage and I remember sitting with my father's mother Regina. It was a very sad trip as my maternal grandmother, Maria, died on the train. I remember my mother getting off the train with some officials at a stop to attend to her burial.

On 27 May 1945 Maria Weiss was buried in Kolin, a small town about fifty kilometres south east of Prague.

The death of my grandmother was a terrible shock to my mother. I remember her sitting in the train and just staring ahead, her eyes red and her lips clasped tight.

The trip back to Bratislava took about one week because there were a lot of derailed train tracks. I remember the train stopping at various stations and the passengers being given edible food.

I remember thinking about the reunion that I was expecting to have with my father. The thought of seeing his face again, of him lifting me up for a hug, brought me much joy on that train journey home. How could I know that my world was about to be shattered, yet again?

---

1   Endearing name for father in Slovak

2   Bread made without yeast, which is what the Children of Israel made and ate, as they did not have time for the bread to rise before they left Egypt. During the eight days of Pesach we only eat Matzah to remind us of this time in our history.

3   *'Hitler Gives The Jews A Town'* a documentary film shot in Theresienstadt in August/September 1944.

4   'Warning Typhoid Fever'.

5   I found the date in papers my mother brought out to Australia.

My mother Helen, aged three, with her parents Maria and Abraham Weiss, 1909.

ברוך הבא

ABRAHAM WEISS U. FRAU
GABOR DREXLER U. FRAU

LADEN SIE HÖFL. ZUR TRAUUNG IHRER KINDER

LONCY UND **JENÖ**

WELCHE SONNTAG DEN 15. MÄRZ L. J., UM HALB 2 UHR
NACHMITTAGS IM STATUS QUO TEMPEL IN TRNAVA STATT-
FINDEN WIRD.

TRNAVA.   IM MÄRZ 1931.   ŠPAČINCE.

Telegramme: Weiss Kapitulská ul. Trnava.

Opposite: *The wedding of my parents in Trnava, 15 March 1931.*

Opposite insert: *The wedding invitation.*

Above: *Aged three, before my first haircut.*

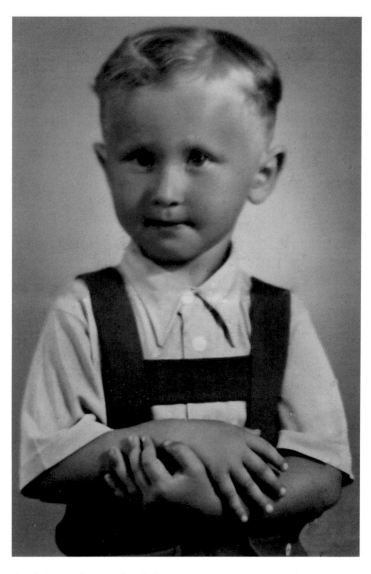

Aged three, after my first haircut.
(Upsherrin is the celebration of a Jewish boy's first haircut).

Above: *My childhood home in Špačince. I was born in this house.*

Left: *Standing next to the original well in the garden of my childhood home.*

Photos taken in 1996.

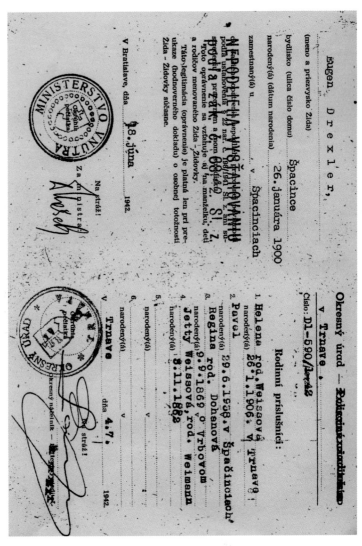

The exemption certificate that protected my father from deportation in 1942. This certificate also applied to my mother, myself, and both sets of my grandparents.

Top: *My identity card in Theresienstadt.*

Centre: *My health immunisation card in Theresienstadt.*

Bottom: *My ration card in Theresienstadt.*

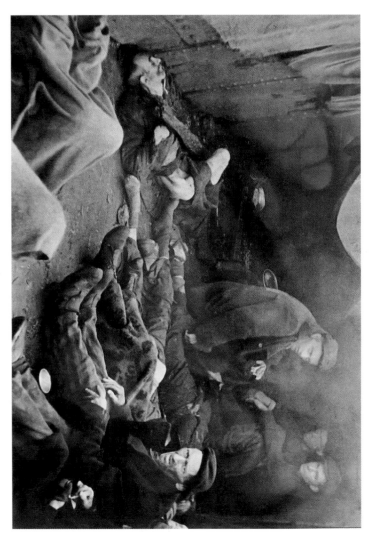

Evacuees from death marches arriving in Theresienstadt, April 1945.

(Terezín Places of Suffering and Braveness 2003)

CHAPTER

III

RETURNING HOME

When we eventually arrived in Bratislava, Walter, the bookkeeper from the estate that my uncle Josko managed, met us at the train station. He took the three of us, my mother, my grandmother Regina and me, to his brother's vacant one bedroom apartment. It was modern and comfortably furnished – paradise compared to the conditions in the dormitory in Theresienstadt and the discomfort of our long return train journey. Josko had organised for food to be there for us, and the three of us sat down to eat together.

Despite our relief at being safe and together, there was a shadow hanging over us. We were saddened and still somewhat in shock over the death of my grandmother Maria. On reflection, I do not know how my mother coped with the turmoil of the sudden death of her mother and her burial in a cemetery in a strange town. In addition she was burdened with the anxiety of not knowing the whereabouts of my father.

During the next two days we stayed in the apartment catching up on sleep and going on short walks alongside the Danube, enjoying the warmth of the sun. On the third day, my uncle Josko arrived to take us back to Špačince. The three of us burst into tears as soon as he walked into the apartment. It was wonderful to see him again and I thought it would not be long before I also saw my father.

It was a beautiful summer's day in June 1945 as we drove through the countryside on our way back home to Špačince. My uncle Josko sat in the front of the car next to the driver while my mother, grandmother and I sat in the back seat. I could hardly contain my excitement in going back to the security of our home and being reunited with my father. I naturally thought, being seven years old, that our home would be exactly as it was when we left it the previous autumn.

My expectations were soon shattered. As the driver opened the gates to our courtyard and we drove in, I saw that nothing was the same. The Alsatian was no longer on the chain; there were no chickens in the coop; there were no ducks wondering around; the stables and cowshed were empty. It was desolate. The three of us, my mother, grandmother and I, got out of the car and when my mother opened the door to our home, it did not look like the home I had left and dreamt of coming back to. My beautiful wooden horse and all my toys were gone; there were no pictures on the walls or photographs of our family on sideboards. All that was there were three beds, a table and four chairs. But, we were home and that was all that mattered.

While we had been recuperating in the apartment in Bratislava, my uncle Josko had been trying to regain possession of our home. When the Soviet Army liberated Slovakia months earlier, Pán Novak and his family had quickly vacated our home and taken all our valuables, including our furniture, back with them to Trnava. Soviet soldiers then occupied the house for a couple of months. After the soldiers left, squatters moved in as the village people did not expect us ever to return.

Josko got the squatters out and arranged to have the house completely cleaned. He managed to get us some basic furniture and crockery, and brought with him a case of apples and some vegetables, eggs and bread to get us started.

I remember Josko sitting at the table that day and telling my mother how his good Christian friends had hidden him to avoid the final Nazi roundup of Slovakian Jews. In the days and weeks that followed our return home, I came to realise that not all Christians in our area were so benevolent towards Jews now. We were not made to feel welcome by the people in the village. Some of them called out 'dirty Jews' as I walked along the streets with either my mother or grandmother. I could not understand this and when I asked my grandmother she explained to me that they resented that we had survived and had returned to Špačince. We were alone in this experience – out of fifty Jews formerly living in the area, we three were the only survivors to return.

As it was the summer school holidays there was not much for me to do. My mother organised our home to make it as comfortable as possible. She was able to rent out the granny flat to a woman with two little children and that gave us a small income. This income was essential for our existence as my mother very quickly learnt that the Nazis had looted all our bank accounts. My mother was very anxious to find out where my father was and made regular trips into Trnava and Bratislava.

Fortunately, my grandmother was able to look after me while my mother was away and I passed the time playing with the children who lived in the granny flat and were about my own age.

My mother told me that the reason she travelled to Bratislava was to be at the station when my father returned. She met every transport of survivors returning from the concentration camps. She told me she always held up a piece of paper with my father's name written on it and she would ask as many men as she could if they had had any contact with Eugen Drexler. She would leave early in the morning for Bratislava and I would wait all day, hoping that when she returned my father would be with her. I was always devastated when she returned alone, but she would reassure me that perhaps the next time my father would come back with her. I dreamt every night of my mother coming back with my father and him looking exactly as I last saw him in Sered.

It must have been about six weeks after our return from Theresienstadt when my mother returned from her final trip to Bratislava. Her face was pale, her eyes strained and her hands were trembling. I had never seen her in such a state. My grandmother and I did not know how to comfort her. My mother sat down and cried. When she calmed herself a little she was able to tell us what had happened. As on previous trips to meet the transports, she was on the station platform, holding her piece of paper with my father's name on it when a man approached her and said, 'I was with Eugen

Drexler'. He then told my mother that they were with other prisoners who all had been subjected to very hard labour for a long time. They were near total exhaustion when they were made to march to Lübeck Bay, where they were told they would be put on Red Cross ships and taken to safety. When they eventually arrived at Lübeck Bay they were rushed by the Nazi guards onto the actual beach when a bombardment by the British Air Force suddenly began. The man told my mother that my father was killed during the bombardment. My mother, grandmother and I cried uncontrollably for a long time. I felt as if my whole world had fallen apart. I needed Tatichko and I needed him now.

Although I had been told my father would not be returning, I could not accept it. I believed he would still return. I continued dreaming of my mother coming back from Bratislava, getting off the bus with my father. These dreams continued for many months.

It would be another half century before I began my formal quest to find out exactly what happened to my father. However, I realise as a much older man, that the search for my father began that day in July 1945.

I was seven years of age when the school year began in September 1945. I felt very sad going back to the local school – I wanted my father to come with me and see me entering second grade. And I could not understand why many of the older children called me a 'dirty Jew'.

One afternoon on my way home from school, I was walking near the river when two older boys asked me to come and join them in their rowing boat on the water. Although I did not know who they were, I thought 'why not', and got into their boat. I enjoyed being with them – they were very friendly and it was fun. While we were rowing, we came across three older boys on the riverbank who began shouting repeatedly to the boys in the boat 'drown the Jew, drown the dirty Jew'. I became very frightened, as I could not swim and I knew that if I was pushed off the boat I wouldn't have a chance. Fortunately, my two companions were very decent and did not take any notice of what the boys on the bank were shouting. They rowed me back to shore. I felt better being on land again but ran home quickly. I was still very upset when I got home. My mother comforted me but found it difficult to explain to me the anti-Semitism that had always existed in the Špačince area. With great patience she explained to me that while my father was alive, the residents in the area who needed him to sell their wheat treated us with great respect. Now that my father was not there with us, many of them chose to forget how my father had helped them over many years. We were not wanted in Špačince any more.

MOVING TO TRNAVA

My mother and grandmother became very uneasy living in Špačince, as they heard that pogroms had been carried out against Jewish survivors living in some of the rural areas. We were only two women and a young boy and had no protection.

Unbeknown to me at the time, my mother decided to sell our home and move us to Trnava where she was born, and where she knew some other Jews who had also survived the Holocaust.

In March 1946 my mother eventually sold our home but for very little money, as times were extremely difficult. My mother, grandmother and I moved into a small apartment in Trnava, which she rented from her good friend, Mrs Jenka Manheim. Before my mother was married she worked for the Manheims in their textile shop. Mrs Manheim was fortunate to be hidden throughout the war. She lived with her son, Richard, who during the war had been sent to England for protection and had served in the British Army. He was in his early twenties. Mrs Manheim's nephews, Sandy Krauss, who was in his early twenties, and Walter Krauss, who was fifteen, also lived with her as their parents had perished in the Holocaust. There were twelve apartments in the shape of a quadrangle. The Manheims lived in the front, on top of the shops. We had a small apartment on one side. There was some grass in the quadrangle where I played with the other children who lived there.

I found it very difficult to settle in Trnava. Life was so different in the town. In Špačince my mother knew nearly everyone and we had a lot of space both in and around our home. My grandmother, mother and I now lived in an older small apartment consisting of a kitchen, lounge room and bedroom upstairs. Downstairs was a toilet and storeroom.

Looking back, I now realise that I had no idea what my mother was going through. She always had tremendous strength but inside she must have been very bruised. She was only forty years old and now had to face the reality of being a widow, and the breadwinner.

My mother continually made inquiries as to what had happened to her sister, Bertha, her brother-in-law Adolf and their small nine year old son, Marcel. They had lived in Vienna before the war, along with other relatives and friends. Eventually my mother found out that Bertha, Adolf and Marcel had all perished in Auschwitz. This was another great loss my mother had to somehow come to terms with.

In spring 1946 my mother enrolled me in the local school, which she had attended as a child. I went into second class primary. Not only did my mother attend the school many years before, the teacher she had in second class was still there and was also my teacher.

By now I had become an avid reader of adventure books and enjoyed playing board games with my mother and grandmother. However, I felt very much alone. It was hard to make friends at the new school.

What I missed most was the presence of my father. I longed for a male role model.

My uncle Josko came to visit once a week and always made sure we had an ample supply of fruit and vegetables, which he had sent from the large estate in Budmerice. After barely surviving on such awful food in Theresienstadt, my body finally began to heal and grow from the fresh food my uncle provided. On school days I would eat a sweet roll and drink warm milk before leaving for school, which began at eight o'clock. Each day my mother would give me a sandwich to eat at morning recess. I found it so strange that when I took out my sandwich there were other children around me who had nothing to eat. Although my mother and I had lost everything and were in poor circumstances, I was disturbed that other children seemed to have even less than me. I felt so badly for them that I would often share my lunch with them.

Every Friday night I went to the Shabbat evening service to say Kaddish for my father. The service was held in a small hall at the rear of the Status Quo Temple in which my parents were married in 1931. At the service I was the only child in attendance, together with fifteen to eighteen men. We had all survived the Holocaust.

To get to the hall I had to go through a narrow cobblestone lane. One Friday night as I entered the lane, a group of youths came behind me and began shouting 'dirty Jew' and threw stones at me. Scared and alone, I ran towards the hall. I turned around to see how close they were when a stone hit me in the temple area just above my eye. I was in pain and confused – I could not comprehend why this was happening to me. I must have looked a mess, with the blood running down my face, as I staggered into the hall. The men were alarmed to see me in this condition and immediately tried to comfort me as well as attending to my wound. I was then able to take my usual seat, next to Mr Koth, who had been a friend of my mother since her youth, and then joined in the service. It was obvious to the other congregants that I was still suffering from shock so two of the men accompanied me home.

Despite being poor, my mother always lit the candles and cooked a lovely dinner for Shabbat on Friday nights. We had cooked chicken with a delicious sauce, hot baked potatoes and vegetables in season, and of course, traditional challah.

My mother supplemented her income (a small widow's pension) by dealing on the black market. She was very resourceful and was able to contact the men from Trnava who were returning to Slovakia from the USA, where they had gone at the beginning of the war to work and provide for their families. She traded in ladies silk stockings, US dollars and Philip Morris and Lucky Strike cigarettes, which the men brought back from the USA.

I remember on one occasion the police coming to our apartment and searching for the goods that my mother traded. It was a horrible, frightening experience. I had visions of my mother, grandmother and me being taken to another jail. Fortunately nothing was found.

My mother suffered extensive trauma from her experiences during the Holocaust: the loss of her husband after only fourteen years of marriage; the death of her mother on the journey home and having to bury her in an unmarked place; and the loss of all our money and possessions, stolen by the Tiso government. She felt lonely and hopeless for the future. She corresponded regularly with her brother Arnold who lived in Wisconsin, USA, as well as her sister Natalie who, together with her husband Ludwig, now lived in Australia. Arnold urged her to leave Slovakia as soon as possible and migrate to the USA. He wrote: 'Loncy, you deserve a better life for yourself and Palko'. Natalie and Ludwig were also willing to sponsor us to come to Australia.

Many years later my mother told me how unhappy she was then and that she wanted to leave Europe. However she worried about how we would fare in an English speaking country. She needed to work to support us and wondered what type of job she would be able to get as she only knew basic greetings in English, like 'thank you', 'good afternoon' etc. But despite her concerns, she took her siblings' advice and started investigating the possibility of emigration. As it turned out, it was easier to obtain a permit to migrate to Australia than to the USA. She applied, and waited for the outcome.

In the autumn of 1947 my mother and I received an invitation from the Jewish Community in Trnava to attend the re-opening of the synagogue. At the end of the war only the shell of the synagogue remained but with the help of the government, it had been fully restored to its original grandeur. To me it was very exciting. I had never before experienced seeing so many Jewish people together in Trnava. The synagogue was overflowing with people, about 300 in total. Many came from Bratislava. I remember lots of speeches by visiting dignitaries and everyone was dressed in their best clothes. After the ceremony of rededication there was a magnificent afternoon tea. This was the only time I remember attending a major Jewish function in Trnava.

My mother and I attended Rosh Hashanah and Yom Kippur services in the newly restored synagogue for the first time in 1947. Shabbat and minor festivals were still held in the hall.

When I returned to Trnava in 1996 with my family, I discovered that the synagogue had just been restored again and was being used as a museum of fine arts. The curator of the synagogue told me that during the communist era the synagogue had been ransacked and for many years used as a grain storage building. It was a peculiar feeling entering the synagogue and finding modern art displayed there in the middle of the sanctuary. In the ladies gallery there were a few remnants of Judaica belonging to the original synagogue, which left me feeling quite uneasy. The atmosphere there was almost haunting.

Arrangements for our emigration were in the hands of the American Jewish Joint Distribution Committee (JOINT). They were based in Bratislava, where we had to travel for an interview. When we arrived at the building that housed JOINT, an American woman with long red hair met us and ushered us into a tiny room that had no seats. No sooner had she closed the door than the room began to move upwards. It was my first time in an elevator! What an experience for an eight year old from the village of Špačince!

When we returned to Trnava my mother showed me a map of the world. She pointed to where we lived in Europe and then to where we would be going: Australia, the furthest continent away from Europe. My aunt Natalie sent photos of her and my uncle Ludwig to us so that I would know what they looked like. My mother explained to me that we would be leaving Europe to settle in Australia, to get away from the past and begin a new life.

My grandmother would not be coming with us, but she was very stoic. She wanted the best for us.

Finally our papers came through. On the evening of 15 November 1947, Uncle Josko took my mother and me by car, together with our three suitcases, to the train station in Trnava. At the station the reality of the situation became apparent. I would never see my grandmother and Uncle Josko again. I cried without restraint. My life had changed from being a small boy living happily with his parents in Špačince and having contact with many relatives and friends, to having my childhood taken away by being interned in Sered and Theresienstadt. The three suitcases were all the possessions my mother and I had between us in the world and we were now leaving for the unknown. If only my father had been with us, life would have been so different.

Parting from my grandmother and uncle was very long and emotional. The final goodbye came when my mother gave my uncle my father's gold fob watch. She had recovered this from a neighbour in Špačince who had hidden it together with a few of our meagre possessions before we were taken away in 1944. I was shocked when my mother handed my uncle my father's fob watch, as this was the only item I had that belonged to my father. All I could see was the sad look in his face when I last saw him in Sered. But my mother was concerned that the watch could be confiscated from us before leaving the country and she wanted it kept in the family.

I was still very upset when we boarded the train. I cried as I sat with my face against the window as the train pulled away from the platform. I was leaving the only life I had known. My mother and I were leaving a graveyard. We were not wanted.

OUR JOURNEY TO AUSTRALIA

The next morning the train arrived in Prague. We took a taxi to a big hotel in Wenceslas Square. I was quite astounded to find that the clerk at reception spoke to some people in German, others in English and to us in Czech. We stayed in Prague for two days. I found Prague similar to Trnava in architecture, with its cobblestone streets and medieval churches and buildings. It was much larger though, and there were more people in the streets; it was all very exciting. We walked up to Prague Castle, which towers above the city and Vlatava River. I had never seen or been in such a huge building. What intrigued me the most about the castle was the guide telling us that in the 1800s, noblemen on horseback would joust against each other in the ballroom which was on the first floor and force one another to fall through the windows to the ground below.

Even as a small boy in 1947, I was very impressed by Prague. My opinion had not changed forty-nine years later when in September 1996 I returned to Prague with Diane, Julie and Michelle. In May 2004, Diane and I again visited Prague and I still think it is a very special city.

The last day my mother and I spent in Prague was devoted to shopping. As my mother could not take any Czech money out of the country, she decided to purchase some special items to take with us for our new life in Australia. She bought two sterling silver Shabbat candlesticks to replace those stolen from our home by the Slovak government during the Nazi era. These silver candlesticks still take pride of place each Friday night on our Shabbat table. She also bought some Bohemian glassware.

After our shopping spree I was extremely hungry. We found a small Bohemian country-style restaurant. Inside, it was fitted out with charming timber tables and chairs, and decorative plates on the walls. I remember being greeted at the door by a largish man with a friendly smile, which immediately made me feel comfortable. My mother ordered a typical Bohemian meal: beef, covered in a traditional sour cream sauce and accompanied by wonderful potato dumplings. The meal was delicious, and my hunger was satisfied. On both my return visits to Prague I sought out Bohemian style restaurants and enjoyed similar dishes to those I had had in 1947.

After two days in Prague it was time to fly to Belgrade. I had never been to an airport before, let alone on a plane. Fortunately my mother had told me that our luggage would be searched at the airport, otherwise I am sure I would have been frightened when two men opened our cases and started poking around in our belongings. Once they had done their job, they closed the cases and allowed us to proceed to the departure area. While we were waiting, I sat against the window and was fascinated to see planes on the tarmac. I could not believe that I would get into one of them, and would go up in the air!

After some time we were ushered out of the building and walked over the tarmac to stairs leading into a small plane. I was very excited as we climbed the stairs, and even more excited when the air hostess showed me to my seat. There were only 12 seats. I cannot remember if there were seat belts but I do remember the feeling as the plane took off – my stomach flipped and turned and I worried that I would be sick. I was somewhat intrigued that the man sitting on the other side of the aisle was slicing salami with a pocketknife and devouring each slice with such relish. Didn't his stomach feel funny too? I was nervous but as the flight progressed my stomach settled down. We flew from Prague to Belgrade, the capital of Yugoslavia at that time. After flying for about an hour we landed and a man representing JOINT met us.

He arranged for our luggage to be brought out and we joined a group of people who were also leaving Europe. A small bus took us all to a hotel in Belgrade where we were to stay overnight. It was the first time I had seen a city that had been severely bombed. Many of the buildings were completely destroyed and rubble just lay everywhere in the streets. Despite my own difficult experiences, I could not even begin to think what life could have been like living in a city where the bombs struck at any time. It was a shocking sight to see.

The hotel was comfortable. All the people in the group sat at the same table for dinner and the JOINT man who was very hospitable looked after us all.

Early next morning we were taken to the train station, where our host bid us goodbye and we boarded the train for Zagreb. Zagreb was certainly different from Belgrade and it had not been bombed. We enjoyed walking along its streets, admiring the large university and the gardens of this small city. My mother befriended a single lady from the group who joined us for the afternoon and had dinner with us before we returned to the station and boarded the train bound for Split.

This time we had a sleeping compartment for both of us, with its own bathroom. It was certainly different sleeping in a bunk bed with linen and blankets as opposed to the train journey from Sered to Theresienstadt when I slept on the floor in the corner of the cattle train with only my small blankets to keep me warm.

I woke up early the next morning; it was already light and I looked out of the window. What an amazing sight. All I could see was blue water. This was the first time I had seen the sea. I became very nervous about our forthcoming sea voyage. It was not long before the train left the coastline and travelled inland again, headed for the port of Split. In Split we made our way to the Hotel Bellevue that the JOINT had booked for the group. The hotel was situated on the esplanade that ran along the whole length of the shoreline.

Split, a seaport on the Dalmatian Coast of the Adriatic Sea, was a very popular holiday destination prior to World War II. The climate was very pleasant, and the scenery was spectacular. The mountains formed a backdrop to the beach along the coastline. The buildings all had an old world charm. As a nine year old boy on his first visit to the seashore I found it overwhelming.

The large palm trees on the waters' edge particularly fascinated me. I had never seen a palm tree before. The only one I had ever seen was on the frieze of my blankets that had travelled the journey through the camps and were in our luggage bound for Australia.

We were supposed to stay in Split for a few days, but our ship the SS *Partizanka* was delayed. Our few days stay stretched to fourteen. Our group of twelve people were the only guests staying at the hotel. We were told by the staff that before the war, the hotel was always full with tourists enjoying the ambience of the hotel and its position opposite the calm waters. The rooms were very comfortable and there were several lounge areas with attractive furnishings.

I became friendly with the only other child in our group waiting for the SS *Partizanka*, a girl who was two years older than I. She also came from Slovakia and we were able to talk in Slovak. We spent hours wandering around the hotel with its many lounges and salons and dining areas. We also explored the port and enjoyed watching the local boys diving into the sea to retrieve coins thrown in by passers-by. This was better than going to school.

Life was so new and exciting for me. I was enjoying the sense of freedom. But, although I knew that I would never see my father again I desperately wanted to share these happy times with him.

The length of our stay in Split allowed my mother a much needed rest. She, along with all the other adults were survivors, and each had his or her own story to tell.

They spent long hours getting to know each other. These newfound friendships and the pleasant atmosphere enabled my mother to relax and have a little holiday. I was so happy to see her relax and laugh. In fact I don't remember ever seeing her laugh until then.

As our stay in Split was longer than my mother had planned, our money ran out. There was no more money to pay for our accommodation and meals. Being very enterprising she made a deal with the manager of the hotel. In lieu of half a suitcase of my clothing, we could extend our stay until the ship arrived. Before leaving Trnava mother had used up some of her Czech money to buy new clothing for me to begin our new life in Australia. It was a stroke of luck for me that she was able to trade clothes for accommodation, as pink shirts and corduroy suits were definitely not the fashion for nine year old boys in Sydney in 1948!

ON BOARD SS PARTIZANKA

At last, on 4 December 1947, the SS *Partizanka* docked in Split Harbour. Our group who had been waiting patiently were jubilant. We boarded the ship the next day and set sail for Australia. Here was a group of Jews leaving Europe – their families, homes, and former lives – and heading to the unknown. Although I was thrilled with the thought of sailing on a big boat, I wondered what my mother was thinking. I just wished and wished my father was there and we could talk about going to a new land together. I really missed him.

The SS *Partizanka* was very appealing and colourful, with a blue funnel with red stars painted on it, and a white upper deck. The top three decks were very wide and wrapped around the ship, allowing passengers to walk around the different decks for exercise. The ship was divided into first, second and third class. Each class had its own lounges and dining rooms. We were in the third class, which was on one of the lower decks. My mother chose a larger cabin housing eight bunks, which we shared with two Italian families; my mother also chose this cabin because it had two portholes, a bathroom as well as a separate toilet. Smaller cabins in third class did not have private bathrooms or toilets.

We were very fortunate with the families with whom we shared the cabin. The husbands had immigrated to Australia two years earlier and had now returned to bring out their wives and children. They were very family orientated and despite the language barriers we made ourselves understood and got on very well.

On board there was a mixture of nationalities including Slovaks, Czechs, Yugoslavs and Italians. We made up an interesting and exotic group of passengers.

Although my mother and I were officially 'third class' we were allowed into the first class section to enjoy their facilities, but we ate our meals in the third class dining room. The Mediterranean style cuisine was completely different from the Hungarian/Slovak cooking I had grown up with. It was a journey of discovery and the new foods were a part of this journey. There was a fixed menu each night. The soup, which was usually consommé beef or chicken, was served from a large tureen at the table. This was a far cry from the 'soup' we had been given in Theresienstadt.

I was intrigued by a new type of food: spaghetti. Twice a week, the distinctive aroma of spaghetti bolognaise, topped with masses of parmesan cheese, filled the whole dining room. I quickly learnt from my fellow diners how to manoeuvre the long spaghetti noodles around a fork.

The first class was located on the main deck, which had a beautiful ballroom, several lounge rooms and recreation areas and a large wrap-around deck. I remember listening to beautiful music being played by live musicians in the ballroom. However no-one ever seemed to dance.

One day after we set sail, my mother became seasick and spent a lot of time in bed in our cabin. She made every effort to come to meals so that I would not be on my own but it was only when we docked in a port that she made it up to the decks. I would have had to spend a lot of time by myself if it wasn't for the friendship I forged with Giorgio, a nine year old Yugoslav boy who was travelling with his mother and grandmother and was also in third class. As we both spoke Slavic languages we were able to converse reasonably well. We had good times together; having the run of the ship we spent our days playing 'ship' from down in the engine room, to the officers mess, and up to the Bridge where the officers were impressively dressed in their official uniforms. Everyone was friendly towards us and we felt very much at home on the *Partizanka*.

Coming from a land-locked country, I had the most incredible feeling when I was on the deck and looking out to the sea, which seemed to me to stretch forever. I wondered where the land would ever start again and how long it would take until we reached it. From time to time another ship would pass us, but it would be far away on the ocean. However, when this happened at night all the passengers would come onto the decks to admire the lights of the passing vessel.

As my mother was so often unwell in bed, the two Italian women in our cabin brought her cups of tea and a little food and often called the ship's doctor to administer different medications to try to stop her seasickness.

When the oceans were calm, and the ship appeared to

glide, my mother felt well enough to dress and also come on deck. She enjoyed the company of other Holocaust survivors who, like us, were looking forward to making a new start in Australia. They formed 'an extended family' which gave the group a sense of security.

In the 'extended family group' were two brothers; their surname was Oblat. I became good friends with both of them. I spent many hours in their first class recreation room playing draughts and dominoes with either one or both of the brothers.[1]

The most exciting part of our trip for me was stopping at the various ports en route to Australia. The ship always anchored in the bay of the respective ports. It was rumoured that as our ship belonged to a communist country it was not welcome to dock at the terminals, and we were not allowed to get off at any of the ports before arriving in Australia.

The first stop was Malta, in the Mediterranean Sea. During this stop additional passengers joined our ship, including a man with a white beard and long white hair down past his shoulders. He was dressed in a long black robe and was wearing sandals. 'Was he a prophet?' I wondered. The next day he reappeared, having had his hair and beard cut and wearing a grey suit, with clerical collar and normal shoes. He was originally assigned a third class cabin but the bursar upgraded him to a cabin in first class, right next door to a rabbi from Hungary who was coming to take up a position with a Bondi congregation in Sydney, Australia. The bursar obviously thought that 'men of the cloth' should be closer to each other!

The rabbi held services on Saturdays; the priest held services on Sundays, both in the same first class small lounge. I attended the Shabbat services almost every Saturday morning. It took me back to the small services that I attended with my father in Špačince.

Our next port was Cyprus, which in 1947 was under British administration. Cyprus played an important part for Holocaust survivors making their way by ships to Palestine. Palestine was also under British rule in 1947 and refused the ships landing rights, thus forcing the ships to go to Cyprus where the survivors were interned in displaced persons camps. In 1948 when Palestine was granted independence, the British left Palestine and the land became known as Israel, the homeland of the Jewish people. Those held in Cyprus were finally able to get to Israel.

The next port of call was Haifa, Palestine, still under British rule. I have never forgotten what happened as the ship sailed into the harbour. Firstly the blue and white Israeli flag was hoisted up the ship's mast. All the Holocaust survivors, including me, became very excited and proud to see 'our' flag flying high. Shortly after the ship anchored in the harbour, the official launch came alongside and the British officials boarded our ship, spoke to our captain and exchanged papers. It must have been about ten minutes later that we all watched as the blue and white flag was lowered and replaced by the Union Jack.

Several new passengers boarded the ship in Haifa. One was a young woman whose husband had been shot by the British during an encounter several months earlier. This woman had received a permit to join her sister in Australia. My mother tried very hard to comfort and befriend this woman who was very distressed.

The next port was Port Said, at the opening of the Suez Canal, where additional supplies were loaded aboard. From Port Said we sailed through the Suez Canal. Seeing people dressed in their exotic colourful clothing going about their daily life was the most incredible experience. There seemed to be sand stretching for miles either side of the canal.

We sailed from the Suez Canal into the Red Sea and reached the port of Aden in Yemin. Many small trading boats approached our ship and offered passengers their wares. The little boats created a floating bazaar. Some were stocked with oranges and coconuts, some with very colourful clothes, and others had figurines, particularly little black elephants with ivory tusks. It was a wonderful sight. The traders would tie a rope to one of the ship's rails and hoist up the goods in baskets. The passengers would send their money back down with the baskets.

Our last port of call was Colombo, Ceylon, also a part of the British Empire. Again small trading boats came alongside our ship. I was intrigued by the large bunches of bananas. Our Italian cabinmates bought one huge branch, which had dozens and dozens of bananas attached to it. They insisted that my mother and I shared the bananas with them as there were too many for the Italian families to eat. I had never seen or eaten a banana before. They had an absolutely beautiful taste and I ate them until I was sick.

After we left Colombo we crossed the Equator and then the weather became incredibly hot. Most of the Italians and Greeks slept on deck. This was before air-conditioning of course.

Among the passengers there were eight or ten Australian men who were returning from a goodwill mission in Europe. One evening they were asked to entertain the passengers with typical Australian songs. It was a wonderful performance and many encores were called for. When they eventually finished I went up to them to say 'thank you', one of the few words I knew in English. The leader of the group handed me a florin coin, being two shillings (now about 20 cents) and said: 'Buy yourself a beer when you get to Sydney'.

1   Within a few years of their arrival in Sydney one of the brothers and his wife became manufacturers of delicious chocolate, hazelnut and other flavoured wafers, under the name of 'Favourite'. When my mother and I visited their factory a couple of times they were very happy to see us, as we were to see them. We reminisced about our voyage on the *Partizanka*.

CHAPTER

IV

LICORICE ALLSORTS

On 7 January 1948 we were told that the next morning we would arrive in Australia. After nearly six weeks at sea, we were excited to actually set foot in our new homeland. There had been tension among some of the adult passengers, exacerbated by the heat since crossing the Equator, and length of the journey. But given that the passengers were from more than six different countries, including Holocaust survivors, the disagreements and misunderstandings were minor.

Next morning, 8 January 1948, the *Partizanka* sailed into Fremantle harbour. The decks were crowded with passengers who were now in good spirits and were cheering. There I was, a nine year old boy. Even though I was as excited as everyone else I could not help thinking about my grandmother and Uncle Josko to whom we had said goodbye several weeks earlier. However, my main thoughts were about my father. Why wasn't he standing next to my mother and me?

Once the ship docked and the formalities were attended to, the passengers began to disembark. My mother and I stepped onto dry land together with a large group of newly made friends. We were now on Australian soil.

As a group we walked together and talked about how we felt about being on land, about the scenery around us. We had not walked very far when we came across of group of shops, one which had the sign 'Milk Bar' outside. Everyone in our group was very curious as to what a 'Milk Bar' would sell. Milk? We walked inside together and were amazed at what we saw. At the same time we were overcome by the deafening noise inside the shop. There were two young men waiting at the counter to be served. On the bench behind the counter we saw long metal cylinders, about the size of two big glasses, which were suspended from what I was later told was a milkshake maker. They were vibrating and making a hell of a noise. We had no idea what was in them. The shop assistant suddenly pulled the metal containers away from their hold, put a straw into each one, and handed them over to the two men waiting at the counter. A great Australian moment.

Fascinated by what we had seen, two of the continental men in our group, who could speak a little English, asked for the same. We all looked as the shop assistant got two containers and proceeded to fill them. First he used a metal ladle full of milk, next he put in some pink liquid and then he used a scoop to put ice cream into each. Then, as we watched, the two containers were put under the vibrating machine and the noise began. We found this procedure very entertaining. This was the first time any of us had ever been in a milk bar and seen a milkshake being made.

Then my eyes turned to the sweet counter. There I saw small multi-coloured squares which I thought had black rubber in between the coloured sweets. I had to try them. With the two shillings I had been given by the leader of the Australian mission on board ship, I was able to buy a small packet of these sweets and received a lot of change. I took one and passed the packet around and we all discovered licorice allsorts, our first Australian sweets.

It was not long before we made our way back to the ship. The atmosphere back on board had changed; everyone was happily sharing their experiences from their short time on land.

The *Partizanka* then sailed for Sydney, our final destination. However it was not all smooth sailing. We had to cross the Great Australian Bight, and there we encountered very choppy seas. For the first time I was seasick and mother and I spent most of the time in the cabin together. I finally understood how she had felt for most of the voyage.

As we approached Sydney there were several farewell parties. My friend Giorgio and I made sure we went to them all to say goodbye to everyone. I was very excited at the thought of reaching Sydney and meeting my aunt Natalie and uncle Ludwig for the first time. At the same time I was sad that I would be saying goodbye to the friend I had made during the six weeks on board.

LESS THAN NOTHING

The morning of 15 January 1948 was beautiful. The sky was blue and the sun was shining. I had never seen such a beautiful sight as Sydney Harbour. Everyone was out on deck to admire the foreshores and the magnificent Sydney Harbour Bridge. It was huge. My mother and I stood together, and I wonder now what she was thinking; I was just plain thrilled to bits!

We docked at the Overseas Terminal Circular Quay. Our luggage was delayed and would not be available for a few hours, so my mother and I left the ship and proceeded through customs, where we had to show our passports, permits and many other documents to the customs official who sat behind a wooden desk. All our documents were in order and stamped 'Passed by Australian Customs'.

Our excitement was overflowing once we spotted my aunt through the long wire fence that was at the back of the customs building. When we finally made contact there was much hugging and kissing. The tears flowed – it had been 11 years since my mother and her sister had seen each other and so much had happened in both their lives since 1937.

I could see the family resemblance in Aunt Natalie. She was the same height as my mother and had similar brown hair. She was slimmer than my mother and I thought she looked a little older.

I felt nervous and wondered what this new country had in store for me. I would have much preferred to have the comfort and presence of my father. However, I was now starting to accept the reality that I would never see him again, although I did wonder what had really happened to him. Would I ever find out?

As we had to wait for a few hours until our luggage could be claimed, Aunt Natalie took us for a walk around Circular Quay and to the Royal Botanic Gardens. On the way to the gardens we stopped at a milk bar. It was a lot smaller than the one in Fremantle. Most of the customers were buying ice creams. My aunt bought me a vanilla ice cream in a cone. This was my very first Australian ice cream.

In our family, we have made it a tradition to have vanilla ice cream cones each year on 15 January to celebrate the anniversary of my arrival in Sydney. When Julie was about 12 years old, she surprised me by bringing a vanilla ice cream in a cone to my office on 15 January saying 'Happy Anniversary'. I have never forgotten that day.

We collected our three large suitcases and proceeded through customs where our luggage was opened and searched. All was in order and we passed through Australian Customs without any problems.

All we had in the world was our suitcases. My mother had two Australian pounds and I had the change from the two shillings, but we also had a huge debt over our heads. My aunt and uncle had paid the 150 Australian pounds for our passage to Australia. My mother knew she would have to get a job very quickly in order to start repaying her sister and brother-in-law.

Many years later, when my mother was more settled and people would discuss what they arrived in Australia with, she would say: 'We arrived with less than nothing!'

THE 'REFO' KID

We were very fortunate that my Aunt Natalie and Uncle Ludwig were settled in Sydney. Ludwig was born in Vienna in 1890 and Natalie in Trnava in 1896. They met and married in Vienna in the mid 1920s. Their early married life was marred by tragedy – they had two daughters who both died in infancy. They never really talked about their baby daughters but had photos of them on their dressing table in their bedroom.

After Hitler's annexation of Austria in March 1938, many dissidents were arrested; among them were Ludwig and his older brother Josef. Natalie worked very hard and used her connections to get them released, but it took three months. Once freed, Ludwig and Josef's parents urged them to leave Austria. By a stroke of luck, the brothers obtained permits to immigrate to Australia. Although Natalie was unable to get her permit at the same time, she urged them to leave as soon as a passage could be arranged, and she would follow once her permit was secure.

However, as a result of the Evian Conference held in July 1938, Australia restricted Jewish migration. Only 300 landing permits for Jews from Austria and Germany were issued each month. It became impossible for Natalie to get a permit to join her husband. By this time Ludwig had arrived in Sydney and, naturally, was very worried about his wife's safety. He urged her to correspond with her brother Arnold in the United States and seek urgent help. Natalie was very fortunate that as well as Arnold she had two sisters, Rose and Erna, also living in Milwaukee in the United States and they were eventually able to secure a family sponsored permit for her to go there and work in their family catering business. It took Natalie two years before Ludwig was able to get a permit for his wife to join him. In 1940 Natalie sailed to Australia on the Mattson Lines, SS *Mariposa*, an elegant passenger vessel.[1]

Natalie and Ludwig rented a two-bedroom apartment in Carrington Road, Randwick, on the top floor of a three-storey 1920s Spanish-style apartment block. From their back verandah I could see the Pacific Ocean. I found this comforting, having just spent six weeks on the ocean. I had developed a great love for its tranquillity.

My aunt made us very welcome in her home, helping us to unpack and settle in. I anxiously waited to meet my uncle Ludwig. He was a skilled craftsman, employed as a designer and cutter for ladies leather handbags. On our first day in Australia he arrived home from work at six o'clock. I remember the moment I first saw him walk through the door – he was about 175 centimetres tall, of medium build, with dark brown hair and a small moustache. He had brown eyes and a ready smile. From the moment I met my uncle, we were friends. Our only problem was language. I spoke Slovak; he spoke German and English – but somehow we made ourselves understood.

While Natalie cooked her speciality, Wiener schnitzel, for our first dinner in Sydney, Ludwig took great pride in showing me his collection of classical music records. The first record he played was the famous tenor, Josef Schmidt, singing *Heüt ist der schönste Tag in meinem Leben* (Today is the loveliest day of my life). My uncle had made leather record binders for his collection and had them precisely labelled.

My aunt and uncle owned a radiogram – a strange contraption that I had never seen before. It had central place in their living room and there was always music in their apartment. At seven o'clock every night they listened to the news broadcast on Radio Station 2BL. As a non-English speaking nine year old it took a long time before I could understand what the radio announcer was saying, but nevertheless I enjoyed sitting with my extended family in the comfort of our new home.

My mother and I spent the first few days after our arrival getting our bearings. It was not only hot in January 1948 but the humidity, which was new to us, seemed unbearable. The only form of fresh air came from the sea breezes.

The first weekend was an eye opener for me. I remember walking with my uncle from their apartment, down the steepest hill I had ever seen, to the oval at Coogee. To me it was a strange sight. There were a lot of men wearing white shirts and pants running and hitting a red ball with a bat. This was my introduction to cricket. My uncle explained parts of the game as it was played. He kept on using the word 'look' as he pointed in the direction of the action. Little did I know that a few years later I would be a celebrated player in the school cricket team.

The next day we all went to Coogee Beach and I experienced the surf for the first time in my life. I walked to the edge of the sea and watched what other boys my age did. They all knew how to ride the waves. I went in a little way and found it was not as easy as it looked! Within seconds a big wave washed over me and dumped me on the hard sand of the beach. I wished my father could have seen this. He would have laughed.

Natalie helped my mother get her first job in Sydney. She found an advertisement in the *Sydney Morning Herald* placed by a Hungarian couple, the Kents, who needed a nanny for their daughter. Mother spoke fluent Hungarian and secured the job. The Kents lived in Norwich Road, Rose Bay. Mother was happy looking after Kristine but the daily travel was a trial. She had to catch a tram from Randwick to the city and then another connection to Rose Bay. But I never heard her complain – she was grateful for the work.

Natalie worked at home making string bags. She was given a huge cone of coloured string, a large needle and plastic handles. She would spend hours making bags for the distributor who would then sell them to the shops.

Ludwig and Natalie were hard working and proud of their apartment. I still laugh to myself when I think of Natalie's habit of covering their three-piece lounge suite with white sheets. The sheets were removed at the weekends, when the lounge suite could be sat on. They took such pride in their possessions, which they had worked so diligently to obtain.

I began school in Sydney at the end of January 1948. On Natalie's advice, my mother bought me khaki shorts and white short-sleeved shirts as I could not have worn my pink or blue shirts to school in 1948. Natalie made sure my lunch was the same as the other boys. Each day for the whole of the first year she made me two white bread sandwiches. One had Polish salami and the other Kraft cheddar cheese. By the end of the school year I was well and truly sick of it!

My uncle had done a 'dry run' showing me how to get to and from school, which was a twenty minute walk from their home. For the first few days my mother walked with me to school and in the afternoon would be waiting for me when the bell rang. The next couple of days she allowed me to walk on my own, but insisted on following me. It was not long before I was walking with other boys from the school.

My first day at Randwick Public Primary School was daunting. I could not understand the teachers or the boys unless they spoke very slowly and directly to me. I had to concentrate very hard on everything. I was the only 'refo' (refugee) kid in the whole primary school and somewhat of a novelty in the playground. When the first bell rang everyone seemed to know that they had to line up. All I could do was follow them. Fortunately, the teachers were kind and helped me find my class line.

I was in fourth class. I had no idea what English grammar was. I could not read or write English properly. However, I found arithmetic easy as I knew my numbers. I could listen to history and geography, and through the pictures in the books I gradually understood the topics.

My first year in Australia was traumatic; I had to go through a tremendous adjustment. I could not believe that being Jewish did not make the slightest difference to the other boys at school. It seemed too good to be true. But it was true. None of the boys at school had any idea of my past life, nor did they have any knowledge of the Holocaust and its effects. They all lived in cottages with gardens and had brothers and sisters. Their fathers worked and their mothers were housewives. They fitted into the norm of 1948 in Randwick.

I was fortunate that I learned English from my classmates. They were very patient with me and encouraged me to play with them. They were always talking and I picked up the words quickly. However, I felt different from them. They came from complete family units and lived in nice cottages and seemed happy and normal. I felt as though I was a visitor at the school with a very unusual background. My mother and I did not have our own home; she worked such long hours and I missed my father.

After school and at weekends, the boys, who lived in various homes in Carrington Road, got together and played in the street itself; there were few cars. This was strange to me, but I enjoyed being accepted as one of the boys.

It worried me that some of the boys at school were playing games of war – they treated it as fun, which I could not understand. The enemy was the Japanese. I learned that some of their fathers had fought the Japanese. Some of them talked about the torture of the Australian soldiers held in Japanese Prisoner Of War camps. I had no knowledge of the war in the Pacific, but in response to my curiosity my aunt enlightened me about Australia's participation in the war against Japan. I was still confused though; the only war I knew about was against Hitler.

I never participated in the war games, but I did enjoy playing Cowboys and Indians!

My mother was working up to seven days a week as Kristine's nanny, which meant that I saw little of her during my first year in Australia. Natalie and Ludwig were good to me. They encouraged me to join in the activities of my classmates at the weekends. I looked forward to Saturday afternoons when the boys would meet at the Clovelly Hoyts picture theatre for the 1.30 pm children's matinee. In 1948 the pictures would begin with three serials, followed by a feature movie – usually a comedy or adventure film. It was often a John Wayne movie, and when he came on the screen everyone in the theatre cheered. There was a lot of laughter and talk among the boys during the interval and after the movie finished. It was during these Saturday afternoon movie sessions that I learned my first lessons about the unique Australian sense of humour.

On Sundays, during the summer months, we went to Clovelly beach where we spent the day playing in and out of the water. In those days no one wore sunscreen or a hat for protection against the sun. My fair skin was not used to strong rays and my back was often very burnt.

Natalie and Ludwig had a small circle of good friends who came from Europe. On Sunday they would meet at each other's homes for afternoon tea and a game of cards. Their friends were always nice to me. My twelve months of exposure to the German language at home and among Natalie and Ludwig's friends gave me a sufficient grasp of the language to make myself understood.

About once a month we joined Natalie and Ludwig's good friends, Mr and Mrs Popper, for a picnic. Mr Popper was a travelling salesman and had a small Ford four-door sedan car. Natalie would make her Wiener schnitzel and pack rye bread, tea, fruit and crockery and cutlery into a basket for our lunch. I was fascinated by the different places we went to: the Royal National Park, the Blue Mountains and Wiseman's Ferry. We would eat our lunch in the picnic area, where there was always a kiosk and Ludwig would take his empty billycan to buy boiling water for our tea. Lunch was delicious. Each of us would take two slices of rye bread and put one of Natalie's tasty schnitzels in the middle.

I was always happy to be part of these outings, but I felt incomplete without my parents by my side. My father was no longer alive and my mother was working hard to make enough money to start paying off her debt to Natalie and Ludwig. Also, the picnics, as lovely as they were, were painful reminders of the times my father took me on his bicycle for picnics in the fields on the outskirts of Špačince. If only I could have those times over again.

On the rare occasion when my mother had a Saturday or Sunday off, the two of us would spend it together. These were precious times. My mother always wanted to know how I was going at school and how I was coping with my new language. I assured her that I was going well. She would tell me about little Kristine and about her parents who worked long hours to build up their furniture business.

If my mother was not working on a Saturday, we would attend the Shabbat service at the Great Synagogue and afterwards she would take me for lunch at a continental restaurant in Darlinghurst Road. There we would usually have chicken soup followed by a beef dish. I remember that while we ate our Shabbat lunch, my mother would reminisce about my father and how he enjoyed the family dinner and lunch on Shabbat, and having members of the family and visitors join us on those occasions. I tried hard not to cry, but sometimes I could not control myself. I still found it hard to come to terms with the fact that my father would never be with us again.

My mother would often say to me: 'Palinko, we are very lucky to be in Australia'. She would cry. I was only young but I knew she desperately missed my father. Secretly, I often cried myself to sleep at night. There was so much that I did not understand about my father's death. Why didn't I have a father like my friends at school?

We found Australians on the whole particularly friendly. But they were interested in the present day-to-day happenings: the weather, sport, especially cricket, and were not at all interested in our past. As we had difficulty speaking English, they would ask out of curiosity where we came from. They really were not interested in the answer. When we said Czechoslovakia that was the end of conversation. Australians in the late 1940s and early 50s were fairly insular. In many ways this was a good thing – it meant we did not have to dwell on our past.

My mother and I found it quite upsetting when we were travelling on the tram and talking quietly together in Slovak when someone from behind would call out: 'bloody refos – speak English!' or 'why don't you go back where you came from!' It was bad enough being singled out and called a 'bloody Jew' in Trnava at the end of the Holocaust, but being called names in our adopted country was frightening.

In the early 1950s when Australia opened up to European migration, allowing many thousands of new settlers to make their home here, a new name 'New Australians' was coined. Thereafter 'bloody refos' was no longer heard as often.

While listening to the evening news in February 1948 we heard that Klement Gottwald, the Prime Minister of Czechoslovakia, had formed a pro-communist government and Czechoslovakia was declared a 'people's democracy' – a step towards socialism and ultimately communism. The country became a satellite state of the Soviet Union.

President Eduard Benes resigned in June 1948 and died a broken man three months later. My mother cried when she heard the news that the 'model democracy' was shattered, yet again. She recalled the late Thomas Masaryk, the first President of the then new Republic of Czechoslovakia and how much the Jewish people loved him.

My mother was eager to improve her English and attended evening classes twice a week at the Maccabean Hall[2], where she befriended several women who were in a similar position to her – alone without husbands and trying to establish themselves in a new land. She began reading the daily newspapers and listening to the radio, slowly improving her English. My mother joined the local library and became an avid reader of English novels.

At the end of 1948 life changed for us again. After a year of living with Natalie and Ludwig, it was time to move on. Hard as she tried, Natalie was not used to having a ten year old boy living with them permanently. So, because my mother was working such long hours, she enrolled me, reluctantly, in a boarding school in Liverpool. She arranged accommodation for herself with an elderly lady in Courtney Road, Rose Bay. This meant that my mother was within walking distance of her work. However, I was over an hour's train ride from the city.

Queen's College Boarding School in Liverpool was a school for girls up to sixteen and boys up to twelve. In 1948 Liverpool was an outer suburb of Sydney. My mother had no choice but to enrol me at a boarding school that was so far away because the fees there were lower than inner-city schools. Nonetheless, she was forced to take a second job at weekends clearing tables at the Sirocco restaurant in Pitt Street, in order to pay my board. It upset me knowing how hard my mother worked so that I could be looked after as well as attend school.

RISSOLES, JELLY AND CUSTARD

Late in January 1949, on a hot Sunday, my mother and I made the first train journey to Queen's College, Speed Street, Liverpool. I was miserable. Each journey with a suitcase at my side represented a loss to me. In 1944 I was arrested by the Gestapo and forced to leave my home in Špačince. A month later I was transported in a cattle wagon to Theresienstadt. In November 1947 I left my home in Trnava for Australia and now, just over a year later, as a ten year old, I was leaving my mother. I knew why we were going to Liverpool, but deep inside I did not want to be separated from her. I am sure my mother felt just as upset.

It took us half an hour to walk from the station to the school. We were silent. Mrs Higgins, the Headmistress, greeted us and took us to her small office. She was a tall, slim, gracious woman with brown hair and brown-rimmed glasses. Today, Mrs Higgins would be described as an 'English Marm', formal and respectful in her approach. She gave my mother three pages of information about the school year.

The boarding school was housed in a huge converted mansion that stood at the end of a long driveway. It was an imposing building, with iron lace balconies. A large garden surrounded the building. I had never seen a house like this and found it quite overwhelming.

There was a tennis court, used for basketball. A separate timber building had been built in the grounds near the house for the classrooms.

My mother and I were in tears as we said goodbye. I did not want her to leave and clung to her for a long time. Mrs Higgins was very understanding and let me watch until my mother had reached the end of the driveway.

She took me to the boys' dormitory, showed me my bed and introduced me to another boy, Brian, who was asked to show me around. The dormitory was different from that in the Boys' Home in Theresienstadt and the one in the Hamburg Barracks that I shared with my mother. This dormitory was L-shaped with twelve double bunks, each with a mosquito net. I had never seen a mosquito net before and wondered what it was for; I soon found out. Brian gave me a tour of the boarding school area. He was also ten and we became good friends.

By the end of the day, the boy's dormitory was full of boys returning from their summer holidays and keen to tell everyone their adventures. There were only a few other new boys like myself.

This was the eleventh major change in my short life to date. I was now exposed to a different way of life. I found it so strange.

My mother promised me she would come to visit me the following Sunday. Realising that I would see her in about seven days made it just a little easier to say goodbye. However, for the first time in my life my mother did not do what she promised. She did not come.

On the Saturday Mrs Higgins told me that my mother had rung and left a message saying she had to work the next day. I was so disappointed. Later I found out that it was the regulation of Queen's College for parents not to visit the first weekend in order to let the children settle into the boarding school.

Mrs Higgins was strict and insisted on everything being perfect. Our shoes had to be polished every day, our grooming had to be immaculate, beds had to be made perfectly, and punctuality was of the greatest importance in our daily schedule. Strict manners and courtesies applied in the dining room at all times. Our knives and forks had to be correctly placed; we had to pass the bread around the table before taking a piece ourselves. When we had finished our meal we had to ask Mrs Higgins politely, 'May I please leave the table?' On reflection, she did a marvellous job in grooming the students. This politeness rubbed off on us; there were few fights among the boys.

For a boy from Europe only used to continental food, I adapted to this new Australian cuisine fairly quickly. The menu changed every day for each week with the main meal served at midday and a light meal, known as tea, served in the evenings. The menu included Shepherds Pie, sausages and onions, rissoles, jelly and custard, baked apple and custard, rice pudding, and vanilla pudding. Tuesdays were the worst. The midday meal consisted of inedible chops in gravy. The chops were all fat and bones. The evening tea was even worse; the tripe was untouchable. Tuesdays I went hungry.

I was curious about the thin milk served in the dining room. Some of the boys told me it was watered down. Early one morning when I went to the toilet I saw the cook outside the kitchen door pouring water into two half-filled cans of milk – the boys were right.

Fortunately the classes were small and my teacher, Miss Anderson, was sympathetic, especially with the funny way I spoke English. She was a young, patient class teacher who was enthusiastic about her job. She also lived at the school and was friendly with the students. I felt comfortable speaking to her, as she would gently correct my English, thus giving me much needed confidence.

I missed my mother. After that first missed visit, she never failed to make the long journey from Rose Bay to visit me every Sunday, even though it was the only day she had off from work. We would go for a walk towards Georges River and then to a milk bar near the station where we would sit in a booth and enjoy a treat of ice cream and chocolate sauce. I would tell her about the new friends I had made. I was worried about a new subject called elocution, which I found very difficult. Mrs Higgins's mother taught it, and was impatient with us all. I could not see why it was so important to position my lips so that the right sounds would come out. My mother was encouraging: 'Palko, you will understand it all in time', she would say.

When it came time to say goodbye she would give me a big hug and I would not let her go. I still remember the sweet smell of Nivea cream on her face. My mother only wore lipstick and Nivea Cream; her face was always so smooth. Her short brown curly hair and her brown eyes sparkled in the sun.

Sometimes Natalie and Ludwig would make the trip to visit me on a Saturday. We enjoyed walking by the Georges River, sitting on the grass and enjoying ice cream. Ludwig told a few funny jokes he had heard at work, but Natalie would always correct him as she thought he did not say them correctly. It reminded me of the picnics they had taken me on in the year I lived with them. I felt good.

One Saturday afternoon when Natalie and Ludwig came to see me, they gave me a big surprise; they brought Walter Kraus as well. The last time I saw Walter was in Trnava in late 1947 before my mother and I left there to begin our long journey to Australia. Walter had come to Australia as an assisted orphan, sponsored by the Sydney Jewish Community. (Walter was about 16.) He was involved in the Zionist Youth Movement in Trnava and I suppose you could say I looked up to him. It was wonderful to see him again. It made me feel happy, and less isolated.

I enjoyed life at Queen's College. My English improved greatly as I spoke it all the time. The students worked and played together. It was not long before I was playing cricket and basketball just like the others.

Mrs Higgins's husband was the complete opposite of his wife. During the week he studied at Sydney University, so we never saw him. But he made his presence known when he was home at the weekends.

He was a real slave driver. On Saturdays he insisted the boys weed the garden. No one liked him because he would never say anything positive to us, such as 'thank you for doing the weeding' or 'the garden looks so nice after all the work you boys have done'. We did not complain while we were weeding, but we would have great fun afterwards mimicking him.

Each term holiday break and boarders' free weekends I would make my own way back from Liverpool to my mother's room in Rose Bay. I would begin by taking the train to Central Railway Station and then from Eddy Avenue would catch the 333 double decker bus to Rose Bay. I was only eleven years old. When my daughters Julie and Michelle were eleven, there was no way I would even let them catch a bus, let alone a train on their own. How the times changed.

I enjoyed being home, despite the fact that my mother worked six days a week. I had a lot of time to kill during the day and spent it walking around the harbour foreshores at Rose Bay. I was particularly fascinated by the flying boats and watched them land on the water and then take off. On Saturdays I would make my own way to Natalie and Ludwig's where I felt at home. I would take them a small present, which my mother bought. Ludwig's eyes opened wide when I bought him a tin of Bensen and Hedges cigarettes. They were his favourite.

At Natalie and Ludwig's I enjoyed spending time gazing at the ocean from their rear balcony, as I had done so often when we first arrived in Australia. One Saturday I spotted the *Partizanka* on its return voyage to Split.

On Sundays when I had to return to Liverpool on my own I would become anxious and felt nauseous. I would have to lie down during the morning until it was time to take the bus to begin the journey back. This nauseating feeling disappeared once I stepped off the train in Liverpool.

It was the school's policy that only boys under the age of twelve could remain there. At the end of 1949 I was already eleven and a half, so Mrs Higgins advised my mother that I could not return in January 1950. I sensed that I would be facing another journey with my suitcase, but where to this time? My mother had, yet again, a new problem. It must have been such a worry for her, although at the time she never mentioned how concerned she was for me. She would never complain; instead she would say to me: 'Palko, God is on our side, he will help us to work it out.'

ANOTHER NEW SCHOOL; ANOTHER NEW PLACE TO LIVE

My mother was now working as a housekeeper for the author and composer, Dr Alfons Silberman. Dr Silberman was on the Board of Sir Moses Montefiore Home and the Isabella Lazarus Home for Children in Hunters Hill. He was sympathetic to my mother's plight and was able to enrol me into the Isabella Lazarus Home for Children. This helped my mother in many ways, including financially. The Home was subsidised by the Jewish Community and my mother only had to pay for my clothing, schoolbooks and pocket money. This allowed her to start repaying Natalie and Ludwig the 150 pounds she owed them, although she still had to work two jobs to do this.

I spent the summer holidays of December 1949 and January 1950 with my mother in Rose Bay. I was lonely; I had lost contact with the friends I had made at Randwick Public School in 1948 and the friends I had made at Queen's College lived too far away. My mother had met a woman in Rose Bay who had a son, Dennis, also eleven years old. Dennis and I became good friends and would spend two or three days a week together. One day we took the bus to the city to visit Dennis's father who worked at Ashers Hotel in Castlereagh Street. It was exciting to go behind the scenes, exploring the kitchen, preparation areas and staff corridors. We felt very important. We also took the double decker bus, making sure to sit upstairs as near to the front as possible, to Watsons Bay, Neilson Park and Bondi Beach. Dennis was very streetwise so he would plan our itinerary. Dennis and I remained friends through our primary school years and years later we were reunited in junior high school. Dennis was a typical outgoing Aussie who had the 'gift of the gab', while I was rather introverted. We complemented each other and had a lot of fun.

During those summer holidays I also learned to swim at Redleaf Pool and spent a lot of time listening to the Davis Cup tennis broadcasts on the radio.

I lived at the Isabella Lazarus Children's Home in Hunters Hill for three years. Although this was the twelfth major change in my life, I now felt more comfortable. To get to Hunters Hill we took a bus to Circular Quay, a ferry to Valencia Street Wharf and then another bus to High Street, Hunters Hill. It was a novelty to be on a ferry on Sydney Harbour. It reminded me of our entry into the harbour on the *Partizanka* on 15 January 1948.

The Home had only just reopened when I began there in late January 1950, and it was quite modern. The girls' and boys' dormitories, bathrooms and locker rooms were separated by Matron's quarters to keep us apart. There was a well-equipped library, study room and a large kosher kitchen, where the dairy area was coded in yellow and the meat area in green to avoid any mistakes. The dining room had ceiling to floor glass windows and doors leading to undercover verandahs each side, where we could play when it rained. There was a large lawn at the front where we played games, particularly cricket and soccer, and another area at the back where there was a children's playground.

Almost all the children at the Home were from single-parent refugee families. There were initially eight boys and four girls, ranging from the age of six to eleven, but during the years I lived there the number of children increased to the maximum of twenty-four. I became good friends with two of the boys closest to my age. Leo Jacobs was ten and Tony Lowy was nine. We remained good friends once we had left the Home and saw a lot of each other during our teenage years, but grew apart as our careers and interests developed in different directions. However, still today whenever we see each other the bond between us is very strong and we reminisce about old times.

We attended Boronia Park Co-Educational Primary School, where we were known as the kids from 'The Jews Home'. The school was approximately half an hour's walk each way. At Boronia Park we enjoyed the family orientated environment. Most of the children came from working class parents, who were involved in the Parents and Friends Association.

I quickly got involved in all the sports. I became famous overnight when, on the first Friday playing house competition cricket, I scored two sixes in a row, giving our team a winning lead. I was the talk of the school until the next Friday's competition when the captain gave me 'opening bat' but I only scored one run.

As time went on I became a reasonable cricketer but was never able to repeat my first match success, but nonetheless I was selected to play for the school. I became very involved in all the sporting activities, including cricket, soccer and athletics. Because of my involvement and the comradery of the boys, I was able to put aside my feeling of 'being different'. If only I could share these new interests with my father. This was a far cry from kicking the red ball in Špačince.

My lack of fluency in English held me back. In 1950 I was supposed to start sixth class, but I was instead put into fifth class together with forty-seven other students. I excelled at arithmetic, history and geography, but battled with English grammar. I struggled on.

The Isabella Lazarus Home was strictly kosher. All the children from the Home had two sandwiches and a piece of fruit for our lunches. But in my first year at the Home, on the day of the eve of Passover (Seder) we were given one hard-boiled egg and an apple for lunch[3]. As I was one of the older boys from the Home at the school, the teachers would seek my help with any problems connected with the children in the Infants Department. On this day the Headmistress called me to her office around midday and told me one of the little children did not have lunch. I was surprised and asked the little boy what happened to his egg and apple. He was so hungry he said that he'd eaten both at recess. All I could do was to give him my lunch and I went hungry.

One of my duties at the Home was to get up early in the mornings and cook the toast for the children's breakfast. I really enjoyed doing this, as I was able to listen to the radio and the hit songs of the day. I would sing along with Guy Mitchell 'There's a Pawn Shop on the Corner in Pittsburgh Pennsylvania' and 'She Wore Red Feathers and a Hula Hula Skirt'. Although I would have much rather lived with my mother I enjoyed being part of the Home environment.

My mother was very concerned about the lack of a male role model in my life. She suggested to the Matron of the Home that it would be good for me to join the local Boy Scouts group. Matron found out where the scouts held their meetings, which was within walking distance from the Home. However, they met at 7.30 pm every Friday. This caused a problem for the Matron since the Home observed Shabbat. However, I was allowed to join the Scouts, as our Shabbat meal was over by seven o'clock. What a pleasant surprise awaited me when I arrived at the hall where the First Boronia Park Scout Troop met. Half the boys were from my school and the other half I got to know very quickly. I felt at ease in the meetings and activities and became involved in the troop.

My mother had moved to Bondi Junction where she rented a room from a widow. She had full use of the kitchen facilities and bathroom. During the school holidays I really enjoyed staying with her in Bondi Junction. We enjoyed going to the movies, particularly comedies and musicals.

The first musical movie we saw was a re-run of *The Jolson Story* with Larry Parkes as Al Jolson. I still enjoy this film as I always think of my mother and her love for 'The Anniversary Song,' a highlight of the film. I realised only later that the words of this song were a link she had to the memory of my father.

TRANSITION TO MANHOOD

Every Wednesday afternoon we had a scripture lesson in the classroom at the Home. Our teacher, Miss Sontheim, made the lessons enjoyable. She taught us about the Jewish Holy days, customs and dietary laws. As Miss Sontheim lived around the corner from my mother in Rose Bay, my mother organised some extra lessons for me in the holidays, which were most helpful. Little did I know that in the same block of apartments lived a two year old girl who in the future would become my wife.

When I turned twelve Miss Sontheim arranged my Bar Mitzvah[4] lessons with Mr Rothfield, who prepared all the boys for their Bar Mitzvahs at the Great Synagogue in Elizabeth Street in the city. On Thursday afternoon I would leave school as quickly as I could, catch a bus to Gladesville and change to a double decker bus to the city and make my way to the synagogue. I had to attend the Youth Service, conducted by Mr Rothfield, each Shabbat. One Shabbat, I was greeted in the synagogue by Mr Rosenberg, President of the Montefiore Home, who invited me to join his family for lunch after the service. I was touched by his kindness; he always had a lot of time for the children at the Isabella Lazarus Home and would often bring us sweets when he visited.

A few days before my Bar Mitzvah I had an oral test, which took place in the boardroom of the Great Synagogue. At one end of the table sat Rabbi Porush looking very stern with his long black beard and a black suit, and me at the other end of the table. It was a scary meeting. I had only seen the Rabbi during the services, but never spoken to him before. He was quite formal in his questions to me, and boy was I happy when the test finished.

My Bar Mitzvah took place at the Great Synagogue on Shabbat Korach[5] on 7 July 1951. I spent that weekend with my mother and we arrived at the synagogue together. My mother and Natalie sat upstairs and I sat next to Ludwig downstairs. Although they were no longer living at the Home with me, both Leo Jacobs and Tony Lowy came especially to synagogue and sat with Ludwig and me to witness my becoming Bar Mitzvah. A few of my mother's newly made friends, together with those of my aunt and uncle were also there. I felt very proud standing on the Bimah[6] in my school suit (a hand-me-down from another boy) and a gentleman's hat. In those days it was mandatory for a Bar Mitzvah boy to wear a suit and a hat. My uncle was supportive but I desperately missed the presence of my father at this milestone in my life. Looking up at the ladies gallery I could see the tears in my mother's eyes. I knew she was proud of me but I knew that her tears were also for her husband.

After the service we went back to Natalie and Ludwig's apartment in Randwick for a delicious Wiener schnitzel lunch. For my Bar Mitzvah I was given two books, and several biro pens. Ludwig gave me five pounds which, in 1951, was a huge sum of money. I was overcome with his generosity. Ludwig was not an emotional person but I could tell that he was very proud.

During the three years I spent at the Isabella Lazarus Home many children came and went. Most of the children only had their mother and quite often when their mother remarried, the children left the Home and went to live with their new family. The atmosphere at the Home was good for me. We were well looked after; I made many friends, some of whom I connected with years later.

At the Home the evening meal was served at 5.30 pm. At the end of dinner I would read the Hebrew short form of Grace-After-Meals. This was followed by the children reading the same passage in English. One evening while I was reading in Hebrew we had a visitor. It was none other than Rabbi Porush. When I had finished reading the Hebrew portion Rabbi began to talk. I asked him politely to be quiet, as we had not finished. He looked stunned but obeyed my request.

By the end of 1951 my mother had repaid Natalie and Ludwig's loan of 150 pounds. She now worked six days a week as housekeeper for Mrs Silberman, Dr Alfons Silberman's mother. Despite working so hard, she had not accumulated savings; she did not have a husband and I was living apart from her (except for school holidays). My mother was very tired and felt financially insecure. Other continental immigrants whom she had befriended wanted to introduce her to their single male friends with a view to marriage and security. My mother was not interested in remarrying.

She maintained that her only love was her husband, my father. By not considering remarriage, her burden became even harder. But my mother kept her sorrow to herself. She had an iron will.

My mother must have expressed her unhappiness in correspondence to her brother, Arnold, who lived in Milwaukee. Arnold urged her to immigrate to the United States and join him, his wife Josephine and my mother's two sisters, Rosa and Erna and their families. During the winter school holidays in May 1952 my mother and I had new passport photos taken with the view of moving to the United States. We discussed the move together and what the possibilities would be for us in Milwaukee. Even though I was only fourteen at the time, I was very apprehensive about packing up and leaving Australia. I asked Mother whether she really thought the family in Milwaukee would give us any more support than Natalie and Ludwig had been able to give us. Since arriving in Australia, my mother had made some good friends and we had adapted to the Australian way of life. I could not see my mother and me starting all over again in another foreign place. I would only be at school for another two years, then I could join the workforce and be in a position to assist financially. After much thought and discussion with close friends, she decided we would stay in Australia. Her decision was vindicated as early as 1955 when Arnold and Josephine retired and moved to Florida.

I was still living at the Isabella Lazarus Home in 1952 and now attended Rozelle Junior Technical High School.

Years later my mother told me how guilty she had felt that I was not living with her during my formative years, but I reassured her that I had been well cared for. I had become quite independent over the three years at the Home, and decided I could look after myself. I wanted to move back with my mother. After four years of living apart and sharing dormitories with many boys, I was so much happier sharing one room with my mother in Llandaff Street, Bondi Junction.

Attending high school opened new doors for me. I now thrived on English literature, and topped the year. Whether it was chemistry, history or even woodwork, it was not hard for me to excel as I enjoyed them all. In 1954 I transferred to Bondi Junior High School in Wellington Street, Bondi. I walked to and from school and was amazed that more than half the boys in my class were Jewish. It was easy to make friends now, but I became impatient with the slow learning process at the school. Even though I was in the A Class I looked forward to leaving the school system at the end of 1954. Most of the boys in my class transferred to Randwick Boys High to go onto the Leaving Certificate (as it was known then) but I was happy with my Intermediate Certificate, and now being sixteen was looking forward to working and earning money so that I could help my mother.

During my high school days I had a variety of jobs. One of these was making chocolate Easter eggs. However, making Easter eggs was obviously not my forte as my touch was not gentle. By trying to bond two halves to make a completed egg, my fingers kept on piercing one half, and the egg would break. So, after a disaster on my first morning, I was fired.

The more successful jobs I had included working in a delicatessen in Macleay Street, Kings Cross, and delivering the local paper. My longest job, and the most enjoyable, was on Friday and Saturday evenings when I was an ice cream seller at the Wintergarden Picture Theatre on New South Head Road, Rose Bay. I enjoyed many of the movies that were shown there. These jobs gave me more than sufficient pocket money. I opened my own bank account and began saving.

During my time at the Wintergarten I became a fan of Humphrey Bogart. My favourite film was, and still is, *Casablanca*. I have a great empathy for this film, as it is the story of displaced persons caught in desperate times seeking the help of good people to assist them in their plight. I never tire of this film and have a copy of it in my library. Still to this day, I enjoy watching it every eighteen months or so.

11 NOVEMBER 1954

I completed my last Intermediate Certificate exam paper on Friday 5 November 1954. On the Saturday I bought a copy of the *Sydney Morning Herald* and following the advice of my school's Vocational Guidance Programme, eagerly scanned the employment classifieds. I cut out three advertisements for junior clerk jobs – the positions were all with insurance companies. First thing on the Monday morning I walked to the nearby local phone box and I rang them and made two appointments. I had interviews with the Norwich Union Fire and General Insurance Company on the Wednesday and began working on Thursday 11 November 1954. I remember the day and date, because in the city there were charity workers selling poppies for Remembrance Day. I bought a poppy and wore it proudly on my first day at work.

I could not afford to buy a suit, but my mother was fortunate to acquire a hand-me-down sports jacket in my size, which I wore with my grey school pants. I was most embarrassed when my mother bought the best quality pale blue sea-island cotton shirts from David Jones. She maintained that it was important to look good, as it would make me feel good.

By this time my mother and I were sharing a room in a boarding house in Moore Park Road, Centennial Park. We had to share a bathroom and kitchen with seven other boarders. In the mornings I had to be very quick in the bathroom before the next boarder would knock on the door. To have a hot shower I needed to put pennies in the slot of the gas heater. I restricted myself to two pennies and got my timing down to a fine art.

Another thing that I will never forget is that we did not have a refrigerator. Instead, outside our room stood an ice chest. The ice was delivered three times a week at 6 am and placed in a metal container outside the side door. It was my duty to rush down the stairs and bring up the ice and place it into the ice chest. However, I had a problem in summer when I overslept and then found that the strong sun had melted half the ice.

My mother was working regular hours as a finisher in a clothing factory in Paddington, which was within walking distance from where we lived. She now felt slightly more comfortable about living in Sydney. She had made some good friends but was still feeling a bit insecure, as she wanted to have her own apartment and some savings in the bank. At that time most of the apartments were rent controlled and passed from tenant to tenant by payment of a lump sum, known as key money.

My mother used her culinary skills to eventually save up enough for key money. She became well known, by word of mouth within the Jewish community for her delicious apple strudel. People ordered these for special occasions. There was no ready-made filo pastry to be bought so my mother made the dough from scratch. I well remember her kneading and stretching the pastry on the large table in our room. The aroma of the strudel baking in the oven in the small shared kitchen pervaded the boarding house. It was suggested that she should open up a pastry shop. The idea was a good one. However, being a single woman my mother did not feel secure in obtaining a business loan, as she would have had to pay high interest rates in absence of collateral. She had only just paid off the debt of our passage to Australia. At times like this we both missed my father. It troubled me to see my mother work so hard.

I was employed as a junior clerk in the fire reinsurance department at Norwich Fire and General Insurance Company in O'Connell Street in the central business district of the city of Sydney. My salary was twelve pounds per fortnight, of which I paid half to my mother. She did not want to accept it, but I insisted. At long last I was able to contribute.

I enjoyed the challenge of learning about the insurance industry. In the beginning my job involved maintaining the locality register. This involved the recording of all risks undertaken so as to avoid having excessive risks in the same area.

Nick Yushenkov, a very worldly twenty-nine year old White Russian immigrant, was my chief clerk. I enjoyed discussing with him the events in Europe and what the future would hold. There were several junior clerks working in the firm who were around my age and with whom I became friendly. We enjoyed having our lunch together and playing table tennis in the firm's recreation room.

I was enthusiastic in my work and was promoted within the first six months. Because of my potential, the assistant manager, Mr Smith, encouraged me to study for the insurance exams. I completed the first two exams in September 1955 and immediately received an increase in salary. I was very fortunate that I befriended many of the senior men in the company, and I realised by talking with them that there was only a limited level of promotion available to me in the industry. I was seeking a more challenging career and was guided by Mr Randall, the firm's accountant. He explained to me the various aspects of the accounting profession and, following his advice, I enrolled in the accountancy course at the Sydney Technical College in January 1956.

In April 1955 my uncle Ludwig had a fatal heart attack. His sudden death created a great void in my life. He was my only male role model. I had felt close to him and he had been very important to me. Unfortunately, his passing changed Natalie's relationship with my mother. Instead of becoming closer, Natalie chose to distance herself from us. I don't really know why. My mother was obviously very saddened by this. Natalie was our only relative in Australia, and my mother and I felt very much on our own again. She survived Ludwig by thirty years and died in 1985 after a few years of suffering dementia.

My enrolment at Sydney Technical College was the beginning of my tertiary education. It was a hard slog, working full-time and attending evening college three nights per week for three hours each night. As well as attending the lectures, I had to be complete assignments for the three subjects every term and I had to pass the yearly exams. I thought at the time my studies would never end, but after four relentless years I was overjoyed to receive my Accountancy Certificate. I was determined and studied further to become a chartered accountant.

It was extremely difficult to get a job in a chartered accountant's office. At that time most positions for accountancy cadets were filled through family connections, and the old school network. I fitted into neither category. My mother was very supportive, but she knew how much easier it would have been for me if my father was with us. I needed his male support. I had no connections whatsoever, but I was determined to gain a position entirely on my own merits.

In May 1956 I gained a position in a four-partner chartered accountancy firm that would provide me with a wealth of experience. I took every opportunity to advance myself within the profession over the next twenty years. I strove for professional independence. In 1978 I felt confident enough to leave my senior position at the international firm of Price Waterhouse & Co and take what was then the biggest step in my life. I started a practice as a chartered accountant on my own, under the name of Paul Drexler & Associates.

1   This was only possible because America was not at war in 1940.

2   The Maccabean Hall was converted into the Sydney Jewish Museum in 1992.

3   During the day preceding the first night of the Passover it is customary from 10am not to eat bread or Matzah (unleavened bread).

4   When a Jewish boy reaches the age of 13 he has his Bar Mitzvah and takes on the responsibilities of an adult member of the congregation. It is customary for the boy to be called to the reading of the Torah (Five books of Moses) for the first time.

5   Korach led a revolt against Moses and Aaron. Read from the book of Numbers.

6   Bimah is the reading desk located on a platform in the synagogue.

CHAPTER

V

NOTHING IS IMPOSSIBLE!

My mother was elated when, at the end of 1956, she had saved enough to pay key money for a two-bedroom apartment in Bondi Junction. It was the most satisfying feeling for us to have our own home. My mother became quite content, taking tremendous pride in her home, and I now had my own bedroom. I helped her by cleaning the apartment, while she did the shopping, cooking and laundry.

It was such a good feeling to have a home and a good position, and to be succeeding in my studies. During the week my social life was limited due to lectures and assignments; however, on most weekends I enjoyed playing tennis, and during the summer often met friends at Bondi Beach. I was an avid reader of novels – mainly mysteries and World War II escape stories. Also my interest in the movies continued. For special occasions I would take my mother to a live musical show at the Tivoli Theatre in the city.

My mother continued her position as a finisher in a clothing factory and now worked regular hours, which gave us the opportunity to have most of our meals together and celebrate Shabbat on Friday nights. Although she talked about day-to-day events, she continually referred back to the Holocaust. She would talk about the things that happened while we were interned in the camps; she talked a lot about

Theresienstadt and its conditions; and the loss she felt when my father did not return.

At times I found it quite irritating, as I wanted to live in the present. But I did take the opportunity to confirm with her places and events that I had witnessed as a child. I queried the horrific conditions in the cattle trains taking us from Sered to Theresienstadt, the conditions under which we lived in Theresienstadt, naked mannequins in the empty shops in Theresienstadt, and events in the Boys' Home. I needed reassurance that what I remembered and witnessed actually happened. This was very important to me. I later regretted that I did not question her further about what she knew of my father's movements after he was deported from Sered labour camp.

Even though I was more settled, and now in my late teens, I still felt very different from my peers. I was a survivor of the Holocaust, and had lost my father when I was six. I now lived with my mother and my childhood growing-up years had been very different from those of my friends and colleagues. I had also lived apart from my mother for four years, which she always deeply regretted. Although this had made me more self-reliant and independent, I felt insecure in many ways. As a young adult, I was now feeling the effects of my lost childhood.

Our way of life was modest. We had to live within our means as we had no reserves to fall back on. My mother was in her fifties. She was still working full time, had great pride in having her own home and had a nice circle of friends. But because of the backbreaking work she was forced to do in Theresienstadt as well as having to work three jobs for us to survive in Australia, she developed a severe case of rheumatoid arthritis. This continually troubled her and slowed her down, but she continued to work full time, take care of the apartment and spend time with her friends.

I turned twenty-one years of age on 29 June 1959. It marked a significant turning point in my life. I had saved just enough money to purchase a small car – a small blue Simca imported by Chrysler from France.

In my early twenties I joined a number of Jewish organisations, including B'nai B'rith Young Adults, where I was actively involved in its committee, particularly in its community work with disadvantaged and orphan children as well as the aged. I had a large circle of friends whom I met through the various organisations. My close-knit group – Ken Falk, Max Obrecz and I – were like extended family. We shared our ups and downs and enjoyed the funny side of life.

In 1962 a good friend of my mother's brought us together with Rose and Manek Etinger. They were also from Slovakia and had both lost their first spouses during the Holocaust. Rose's maiden name was Drexler and she was a third cousin to me on my father's side. We became very good family friends and enjoyed celebrating Pesach[1] and Rosh Hashanah together. We celebrated First Night Seder[2] at their home and Second Night Seder at our home. My mother felt extremely happy after our first Seder with our new family. However, she did not realise what was in store for her. The following day at work, I received a telephone call from the police informing me that my mother had been involved in an accident. She had been hit by a car while crossing the road in Bondi Junction and was in the Emergency Ward at Eastern Suburbs Hospital. She had suffered a broken pelvis.

She had to spend the next three months in hospital. My mother, at fifty-seven years of age, remained determined; she had to learn to walk all over again. Once on her feet she spent a month recovering at the Sanitorium Hospital at Wahroonga.

The effect of my mother's accident was that she could not continue working full time as a finisher, although her employer was happy to have her work for them on a part-time basis. My mother had always been a great optimist; she believed that nothing was ever impossible. Because of her amazing strength I was naïve enough to think that she could go on forever. But she was ageing and her health since her accident was deteriorating. Her rheumatoid arthritis had worsened and she was under constant medical attention. The reality of this was starting to hit home for me.

My interest in music, theatre and the arts provided the challenge for me to form the Friends of the Israel Philharmonic Orchestra Younger Set (IPO Younger Set). I was President of this group for two years during which time gifted musicians were invited to perform at functions, an active drama group was established and numerous cultural and social functions took place. Knowing that so many young adults met their partners while attending functions at the IPO Younger Set gave me tremendous satisfaction. But most importantly, it was at one of these functions that I met my future wife Diane.

Meeting Diane was the beginning of the most wonderful change in my life. We were introduced through very good mutual friends, Kay and David Meltz, at an IPO Younger Set musical evening in June 1971. I was instantly attracted to her beautiful smile and the sparkle in her eyes. We had both experienced losses in our young years, which I felt drew us together.

Diane was an only child who lived with her father, Howard Gray, in Killara on the upper North Shore. Her mother, Cara Esther Gray, had died suddenly from a cerebral haemorrhage six years earlier when Diane was only sixteen. Diane kept herself busy – working full time, studying for her Accountancy Certificate at evening college as well as looking after the household – but even though she was coping well on the surface, it was painfully obvious to me and to her close friends that she was still grieving for her mother.

Diane and I dated for three years, during which time I made countless journeys to the North Shore and felt that the amount of money I had paid in tolls nearly paid off the Sydney Harbour Bridge!

Together we organised our wedding day, which was on Sunday 13 January 1974. We chose a lunchtime wedding at the Boulevard Hotel, William Street, Sydney, where we had both the Chuppa[3] and the luncheon reception. The late Rabbi Dr Alfred Fabian, who was a school friend of Diane's father, conducted the ceremony. Diane and I were very much in love when we married. On that day we began then the most wonderful partnership which, thirty-five years later, is stronger than ever.

My mother always wanted to go the USA to see her family and to return to Slovakia for a visit. However, she said she would not go until I was married. So in 1976, aged seventy, my mother, after much persuading and detailed planning, embarked on a trip to New York to stay with her eldest sister, Hermine, who was seventeen years older. Their reunion was an extremely happy one.

Slovakia was still behind the Iron Curtain when my mother visited my uncle Josko, who had now retired and was living in Bratislava.

Josko took my mother back to Špačince and also to her place of birth, Trnava. I expected my mother to relate all the details of what she saw in Špačince and Trnava. However, on her return to Australia she flatly refused to talk about her trip to Slovakia. Her only comment was: 'It was all grey; what have they (the communists) done? She was so disappointed that she had returned there, although she was pleased to see that my uncle was reasonably healthy and was able to live comfortably on a government pension.

One great thing that happened on my mother's trip to Slovakia was that my uncle returned to her my father's gold fob watch, which she had left with him in

November 1947 before we boarded the train for Prague. When she handed it over to me, I felt my heart leap. I ran my fingers over it and sensed that he was watching over me.

—⊬—

One Sunday morning in 1980 when I was outside on a ladder preparing a window for painting, Diane came outside and said that she had a funny feeling she was pregnant. For a fleeting moment I lost my balance and nearly fell off the ladder. We were overjoyed when Diane's pregnancy was confirmed later that week.

Our first born, Julie Cara, entered the world on 16 January 1981. I cannot adequately describe the feeling of holding Julie in my arms; she was beautiful. Thoughts flashed through my mind of how lucky I was to have a precious daughter. If Hitler had had his way, I would not be here, and neither would Julie.

My eyes were filled with tears as I longed for my father to be there to share this moment with me. But despite this pain, both Diane and I were ecstatic; we had been blessed with a perfect baby daughter. I now knew that my mother was right and that nothing was impossible!

Proof of this was the birth of our second daughter, Michelle Louise, twenty months later on 14 September 1982. Our happiness at now having two daughters could not be described. We were truly blessed.

When Julie and Michelle began to attend Mt Zion Kindergarten and then the Emanuel School, I made a point of taking them there each morning. We played games in the car, such as counting how many buses were on the road, and they told me all about their friends and activities at school. Those days were very special.

Life changed dramatically for our family when my mother suffered a stroke at our home on Yom Kippur (Day of Atonement) 1986. She spent time in Wolper Hospital recovering and her doctor advised me that it would be better for her to be transferred directly from Wolper to a nursing home. I flatly refuted his advice. I maintained that with our help she would fully recover from the stroke.

Once my mother was back in her own home we did everything possible to make her comfortable, attending to her meals, provisions, washing and medication. My mother, being a great optimist and a survivor, did recover. It was so gratifying to see her play with the girls again.

At the time I did not realise the longer-term effects of the stroke my mother had suffered. It was only a matter of another two years until her mental health began to rapidly deteriorate. Eventually, on the advice of her doctor, we had her assessed by a specialist. She was suffering from dementia. Diane and I had become very stressed as we were attending to her three times a day to make sure she ate and took her medication. We kept on denying the reality that eventually we would have to place her in a nursing home.

In August 1989 it became a necessity for my mother to move from her apartment in Bondi Junction to the newly opened Dementia Section, at the Sir Moses Montefiore Home, Hunters Hill. The irony is that the new building housing the Special Care Unit stands on the very site of the former Isabella Lazarus Home for Children, where I lived for three years from 1950 to 1952.

This was an extremely difficult time in my life. I felt so guilty for moving my mother into the Special Care Unit at Montefiore. When she first moved there, her condition somewhat improved due to the activities organised by the diversional therapists. There were short periods when she seemed perfectly normal and this made me think that it would not be long before I could take her back to her own home. But I had to come to terms with the truth that her mental condition was deteriorating.

My mother had been through so much suffering in her life. I remember her devastation at being told that my father had been killed. Why was this happening to her now when she should be enjoying her grandchildren? It took me eighteen months to accept the reality that my mother would never be able to return to her own home. The process of clearing out her apartment in February 1991 had its effect on my health. On the last day of clearing out I suddenly could not breathe and had to sit down on the floor. I was frightened; I could not understand what was happening to me. It took me a while until I felt I had sufficient strength to get up, and with Diane's help we slowly walked down to our doctor who was fortunately only a block away.

After he examined me he explained that I was suffering from acute stress and was grieving about the loss of my mother as my mother, and as I could no longer communicate normally with her, I was grieving as though she had died. He very sympathetically explained to me that I would again grieve for her when she would physically die. He gave me medication to ease the effects of the stress.

RECORDING FOR SPIELBERG

In 1985 after the worldwide celebrations to mark the fortieth year of the liberation of the concentration camps, Diane encouraged me to write my story. She would say the same to my mother. Neither of us listened to her. Early in 1995 it was announced that Steven Spielberg was to establish the Shoah Foundation. The objective of the Foundation was to interview all Holocaust survivors worldwide and video their testimonies. Diane urged me to contact the Sydney organisers and arrange for the filming of my story.

I was fortunate that I felt comfortable with my interviewer, Shirley Eisenberg. She came to talk to me at my home before the interview, which set me at ease. The interview took place at home early in March 1995. The process took about three hours and I was asked to talk about my life from childhood to the present and the way that the Holocaust affected me. At the end I was emotionally drained.

During the next week I felt disturbed and my mind was in turmoil. I had frightening nightmares where I was desperately searching though concentration camps for my father. I searched through rows upon rows of emaciated men in striped uniforms, but I could not find him. During the day I kept on thinking about my father. If only I could see him and tell him how much I have missed him these past fifty years. If only he could be a part of my life now and enjoy his granddaughters. What really happened to my father? Would I ever find out?

Eventually the nightmares subsided and I began to feel a great sense of relief. I started to make notes about the frightening days of my Holocaust childhood. I talked at length to Diane about all the incidents that had now come back to me and that I had forgotten about until being interviewed for the Shoah Foundation video. Diane suggested that I should document everything and write the story of my life.

CONFRONTING YAD VASHEM

Upon reflection now, it seems quite significant that shortly after I recorded the Shoah Foundation video, we made our first trip to Israel in March 1995. In order to see as much of Israel as possible in the short time we had, we arranged to do an eight-day private tour. Our tour finished in Jerusalem where we stayed an additional six days. Visiting the Western Wall and the Old City were powerful experiences. I had seen countless pictures but never imagined that I would ever be there in person.

At Yad Vashem, I found the large graphic images of the Holocaust quite disturbing. They reminded me of the films taken on the liberation of the death camps that I saw at the movies in Trnava after the end of World War II. I was deeply shocked when I saw those films as a young seven year old and their impact has never left my mind.

Visiting the Hall of Remembrance, the memorial to all the camps, a dark and brooding place with the eternal flame rising up from the floor, and seeing Theresienstadt spelt out in huge letters, left a deep impression in my mind. It brought back memories of fear, hunger and cold. For a second I saw myself walking in the icy cold from the Boys' Home to the Hamburg Barracks to see my mother.

At the Central Archives office I filled out a 'Page of Testimony' for my father. I was shown how each testimony has its own drawer in the huge cabinets, as though those who did not survive, like my father, had their own resting place. It was like a cemetery.

Julie and Michelle were as deeply affected as Diane and I by the powerful message of the Children's Memorial. The structure of the Valley of the Lost Communities as well as the serenity of the Avenue of the Righteous moved us all. It was a powerful experience for us to be in Israel over Pesach (Passover). Our hotel was just around the corner from the Great Synagogue where we attended the service on the first day of Pesach.

The most enjoyable part of Pesach was spending the first Seder night and the next two days with our close friends, Ken and Edith Falk and their three sons, Joel, Roy and Tom. Ken was my best man at our wedding in 1974. In 1976 he settled in Israel where he met Edith, whose family had migrated to Israel from Morocco. It was very pleasing to see how happy Ken was; with great pride he showed us Jerusalem, his city.

On returning home on 29 April, I told Diane that I now knew I had to return to the country of my birth, Slovakia. I wanted to show Diane and the girls my place of birth. My mind was filled with questions of my past. What was I going to find there after fifty years? Would I be able to find any trace of my father's journey since the last time I saw and kissed him in December 1944?

1   Pesach (Passover) commemorates the Exodus from Egypt and
    freedom from slavery.
2   Seder means order. It includes symbolic foods and the reading of the
    Haggadah (the story of the Exodus).
3   Chuppa is the canopy under which the bride and groom stand during
    the ceremony. It symbolises the home they will build together.

Top: *Natalie and Ludwig Flusser, Sydney 1948.*

Bottom: *My mother and me, Sydney 1948.*

Aged fourteen, 1952.

Aged twenty-one, 1959.

Opposite: *Diane and I on our wedding day, 13 January 1974.*

Above: *My mother Helen on our wedding day.*

Diane's father Howard Gray on our wedding day.

Top: *My mother with Julie, aged three, and Michelle, eighteen months, in 1984.*

Bottom: *Michelle's Bat Mitzvah together with my mother, 26 August 1995.*

Top: *With my newfound Drexler cousins Eli and Pat, 2004.*

Middle: *Julie's graduation, 20 April 2004.*

Bottom: *Michelle's graduation, 8 April 2005.*

CHAPTER

VI

RETURNING TO MY PAST

In 1996 Diane, Julie, Michelle and I embarked on the most significant journey of my adult life. When I arrived in Australia in 1948, I never expected to return to the place of my birth. Fifty years later I had a tremendous need to do so. I needed confirmation of my disturbed youth. I had to see where it all began.

On Monday 23 September we observed Yom Kippur (Day of Atonement) in Budapest, attending the service at the refurbished Dohany Synagogue. We then travelled from Budapest to Bratislava, arriving on the Wednesday. After checking into the Forum Hotel in the centre of Bratislava, I telephoned the caretaker of the Jewish Cemetery Trust to confirm our appointment, which I had made with her prior to leaving Australia. I longed for a connection with my family. I wanted to visit the graves of my grandfathers, both of whom had died in 1938. My father's father had died shortly before I was born on 29 June 1938; therefore I was given his name, Gabriel, as my Hebrew name. My mother's father, Abraham, had died a few months after my birth.

Before we left Slovakia in 1947, my mother and I had visited their graves. Mother never thought either of us would return.

Diane, the girls and I, took a taxi to the cemetery and were warmly greeted by the caretaker, who looked quite worried. She had been unable to find either of the graves in the Neolog or the Orthodox Cemetery situated next door. When I showed her the photos I had of my grandfathers' headstones, she said that as both headstones were inscribed in German only, without any Hebrew inscription, they would be in the Jewish section of the Blumfield cemetery. (Bratislava, although the capital of Slovakia, was very much under German influence in 1938, thus explaining the German inscriptions on my grandfathers' headstones.) Unfortunately the cemetery was now under liquidation, a 'nice' term for 'no longer in existence'. I was quite disturbed that the cemetery was now to be bulldozed despite the fact that it housed the graves of those who had died so recently – in the case of my grandfathers, only fifty-eight years ago.

The caretaker located the grave of Jozef Drexler, my uncle, and my father's younger brother. He died in 1978 aged seventy-five years, and was buried in the Neolog cemetery. The cemetery was in an appalling state. There were no distinct paths to follow, the grass was knee high and most of the inscriptions on the headstones were illegible and overgrown with ivy. The caretaker led us through the wet grass to a little clearing and there, in the middle, was my uncle's grave.

It was in near perfect condition, the grass having been cleared around it. There were three Yahrzeit[1] candle containers near the headstone, obviously brought by friends of my uncle, probably on Yom Kippur. I was touched to see how well his grave was kept compared with all the others in the cemetery.

In my mind I could clearly see my uncle in our home in Špačince, sitting at the family Shabbat table and talking to my father about the wheat industry. That was at least fifty-three years ago, before our lives changed.

I said Kaddish[2] and stood and reflected a little more. Then Diane, Julie, Michelle and I walked hand in hand back through the wet grass to the cemetery entrance, where I thanked the caretaker for all her help. This visit to the cemetery was my first step in revisiting the past.

Early on Thursday 26 September 1996 – a cold and cloudy day – we left the Forum Hotel, bound for Špačince, the village in which I was born.

The visit to the house where I was born was very emotional. I remembered the happy times I had with my father and the very short time my parents and I were able to spend as an ordinary family. I felt overwhelmed by the immediacy of the past.

In silence we drove the seven kilometres from Špačince to Trnava, the town where my mother was born, educated and worked until her marriage to my father in 1931. Fifty years later I was again in the town where my mother and I were forced to live for two unhappy and unsettling years of my childhood.

Stefan, our driver, dropped us at the entrance to the cobblestone town square. I looked around and to me it seemed as though nothing had changed. Hviezdoslavova Ulica, the street where my mother and I lived during 1946 and 1947, was dreary. The small block of apartments at number eleven and the quadrangle behind was very neglected. I showed my family the door to what had been our apartment and explained the layout inside. How surreal it all appeared to me. The Holocaust had changed Europe but the fabric and chemist shops in the front of the apartments were still there and continued trading.

Trnava was originally known as 'the Town of Churches'. The churches, emptied during the forty years of communism, were now in the process of being refurbished. I was pleased to see them being brought back to life.

I was anxious to see the house at 28 Kapitulska Ulica where my mother was born. When we found it, I was saddened to see how neglected it looked. We didn't stay there long. We wandered down the main street and to our amusement saw a sign that read 'Kangaroo Burger' above a burger shop. Gone were the coffee houses of 1947. Where were the fashion boutiques and the huge Bata Shoe Shop that I remembered?

Trnava was a walled town. As a small child I remember visiting someone who lived just outside the wall in what was then the villa district. All the villas then were single-storey homes with beautiful gardens with multi-coloured flower beds facing the street. How communism had changed this district. Instead of villas, there were now grey dreary six-storey apartment blocks all in a row. What had happened to the numerous food stores where my mother would buy rye bread, cottage cheese and pickled cucumbers? I felt uncomfortable in this town where my mother had enjoyed her childhood when there was a vibrant Jewish Community. Now there was nothing. I felt empty, and was pleased to leave Trnava behind.

For a complete change we had then booked three days in the High Tatras. My mother used to speak about the High Tatras where people went for holidays to enjoy the walks in summer and skiing in winter. This was my opportunity to see the area she had spoken about for myself.

The only way we could get to the High Tatras was by train. That was an experience in itself. On Friday morning, 27 September 1996, we boarded the train from Bratislava to Poprad, which stands at the foot of the Tatras. We settled into our first class compartment, which was very comfortable. At first the journey was very quiet and we all relaxed, reading our books. At various stops en route large numbers of teenage schoolboys boarded the train on their way home for the weekend. They boarded the first class carriages and crowded in the corridors. Each group was in competition with the others, shouting at the top of their voices. The guard lost complete control of the situation. We felt quite threatened, as we did not know where this disruption was leading. What horrified me most was at each station we stopped there were policemen on the platform with huge leashed dogs wearing muzzles. My mind flashed back to scenes from the cattle wagon into which my mother and I were crammed on our journey from Sered to Theresienstadt.

At one of the stations two young policemen boarded the train and opened each compartment door, looking at the occupants. When they opened our compartment door the first policeman looked straight at Julie, pointed to her and shouted 'Passport'. I froze. I showed him my passport first. He shook his head and pointed again to Julie. He looked at her passport, looked at her, and again at her passport. He turned to the other policeman, uttered a few words in Slovak and almost threw Julie's passport at me, then stormed out of our compartment and closed the door. He was obviously looking for someone else. During those short minutes while he was looking at Julie's passport I had visions of her being taken by the policemen off the train at the next station, never to be seen again! This was 1996 not 1944; what had I subjected my family to?

After this, Julie went completely white and sat in silence for the remainder of the journey. As we approached Poprad Station we saw several policemen with muzzled dogs standing in strategic points on the platform. My heart began to beat very quickly, I felt frightened and wondered what we had got ourselves into by coming to the High Tatras. We quickly alighted from the train and headed straight for the taxi rank, piling into the first taxi as quickly as we could. The strangest contrast then took place. As the taxi left Poprad heading for Novy Smokovec, I began to breathe normally again. There were no policemen with dogs to be seen anywhere, only tourists.

This holiday part of our trip was wonderful. Together with Diane's cousin, Veronica Langstadt, her partner Ezio and their two year old son Giorgio who came from

Padova, Italy, to join us, we enjoyed many walks and breathing in the glorious fresh mountain air.

Our day train journey from Novy Smokovec to Prague was most interesting. The Slovak countryside was bare and the farmhouses looked neglected. Once we crossed the border into the Czech Republic the countryside changed completely. The land was green and the farmhouses very well maintained. I now felt very much better. This train journey was very relaxing – a complete contrast to the one from Bratislava to Poprad just a few days earlier. It was already dark when the train finally stopped at Hlavni Nadrazi, the main train station of Prague, and I felt very happy to be in Prague. We had arranged to be picked up at the station and taken to U Zlate Studny, the hotel where we were to spend the next eight nights.

RETURNING TO TEREZÍN

I was anxious to return to Terezín. I wanted to walk the streets where I had walked in fear, as a young boy, fifty years ago. I had to confirm that I had actually been a prisoner there. Was the Boys' Home still there? Were the Hamburg Barracks still standing? I needed answers to so many questions that had occupied my mind for all those years. What would I find? My mind was so confused that I made something of an error by asking the Jewish Travel Bureau in Prague the best way of visiting Terezín. On reflection we should have taken a taxi there ourselves instead of joining a group of eight in a mini bus accompanied by a guide. There was something about the way the guide began talking on the journey to Terezín that immediately annoyed me. He emphasised repeatedly that he was a learned university professor. What annoyed me most was that he spoke with a strong German accent and had an aura of authority. He lectured us for the entire one-hour journey.

On arrival at Terezín the first stop was the Small Fortress where we spent nearly two hours. From where the bus stopped we had to walk along a path, which was in the middle of the 'Cemetery of Victims' through a gate that had the words ARBEIT MACHT FREI (Work liberates) written above it. During the Holocaust the Small Fortress was a Gestapo prison for criminals, prisoners of war and those who had committed 'crimes' in the ghetto. Now it served the tourists as a museum of terror. It had been meticulously reconstructed reproducing torture chambers, solitary cells and execution area. It was hideous.

Before we got back on the bus to drive the short distance to the ghetto, I explained to the guide that I was a child survivor of Theresienstadt and that my mother and I lived in the Hamburg Barracks. I told him how anxious I was to see it again. He assured me that we would definitely go to the barracks. We drove straight to the museum, which was the original Boys' Home where I lived before I went to the Hamburg Barracks. We were immediately directed to the auditorium upstairs where we saw excerpts of the propaganda film *The Führer Gives A Town to the Jews*. Thank goodness the world never saw this film. Everything about it was false.

The exhibits in the museum were artefacts from various concentration camps, not specifically from Theresienstadt. At one point I was somewhat shocked to hear an American woman say to a guide 'I wonder how the people felt who lived here'. I was tempted to approach her and speak of my experiences but decided not to as I thought I would become too emotional.

The tour included lunch at a restaurant near the museum. This idea was totally foreign to me. How could there be a restaurant in the concentration camp where I had been imprisoned? My mind came back to the present, realising that now in 1996, Terezín was a small town. I went with the flow but it took so long to be served that I left the table several times and walked up and down the street, deep in thought. I remembered elderly people walking aimlessly; two men pushing a cart with a dead body covered with a black blanket; and children looking on curiously.

Eventually our tour guide gathered our group of twelve and we boarded the mini bus. I asked the guide whether we would now pass the Hamburg Barracks, where I lived with my mother in 1944–45, and he assured me we would. We drove through the streets and headed to the crematorium and cemetery without stopping at the Hamburg Barracks.

At the crematorium the guide's unemotional and insensitive manner continued to irritate me. I found his assurance 'that the ashes of camp victims were buried according to nationality' quite unbelievable. My own research has since revealed the truth: over the years to 1944, the many thousands who died in the ghetto were cremated and their ashes were stored in small cardboard boxes. The Germans decided to get rid of the ashes by dumping them into the river[3].

The area where the crematorium was situated was all in pristine condition. To see Yahrzeit candles burning at the open doors of the ovens, to me appeared to be 'a show'. It wasn't real – it was just one more emotive ploy to impress the tourists.

The guide made us hurry, as he was anxious to get going back to Prague so as to avoid the afternoon traffic congestion. I was finding it very difficult to reconcile the events of fifty years ago with the way it is portrayed for tourists today, and resented the feeling of being a tourist in this place where my own story was part of its history.

I became very angry with the guide, this time emphasising that I had spent time here, in the Theresienstadt camp, and I wanted to go to the Hamburg Barracks. 'We already passed there', he replied. 'But we did not stop,' I retorted. 'There is nothing to see there – they are locked until restoration begins, which will be later this year'. His answer was not acceptable to me and I demanded that I be taken to the Hamburg Barracks and allowed to get out and see them for myself. He could see the anger in my eyes and immediately instructed the driver to return to Bahnhofstrasse and stop at the Hamburg Barracks.

As I got off the minibus I felt the weight of the world on my shoulders. I was back at the gate that I had passed through many times all those years ago. It was eerie, looking up at the window of the small dormitory where my mother and I lived during our internment in Theresienstadt. Memories came flooding back. I felt extremely sad and yet relieved that, despite everything, my mother and I had survived. I cannot quite describe what happened next, but somehow the weight just lifted from my shoulders. I began to cry internally. After calming myself, I felt ready to move on, but I remained silent, deep in thought, for the entire journey back to Prague.

We spent the next few days absorbing the magnificent city of Prague. I became completely obsessed with the old city, particularly the restored old Jewish Town of Josefov that is a very small quarter within Prague.

In 1942 the Nazis established the Central Jewish Museum to which were brought art objects from the 153 Jewish communities and synagogues of Bohemia and Moravia, all destroyed by the Nazis themselves. The Nazis intended to have a 'Museum of the Extinct Race', exhibiting the 'Precious Legacy'[4]. The Precious Legacy is now displayed in the restored four synagogues: the Old-New, Maisel, Pinkas and Klaus synagogues in the old Jewish Quarter.

In stark contrast to the magnificence of the items in the synagogues, housed in the Ceremonial Hall – the former headquarters of the Chevra Kadisha (Burial Society) – is a heart-rending collection of 4000 simple drawings done by children imprisoned in the Theresienstadt concentration camp. Fifteen thousand Jewish children under the age of fifteen entered its evil portals; only a few like me survived.

The oldest Jewish cemetery in Prague is situated behind the Ceremonial Hall and contains 12,000 persons buried there, one on top of another, twelve layers deep due to of lack of space. The great Rabbi Loew, a former Rabbi of the Old-New Synagogue, was buried here in 1609.

We attended a Friday night service in the Old-New Synagogue. I sat in the main part of the synagogue separated by a brick wall behind which Diane, Julie and Michelle sat. They could only see into the main sanctuary through the small spaces in the wall. We spent a whole day exploring the magnificent Prague Castle, which I remembered so well from my first visit with my mother as a nine year old boy in 1947, before we left Czechoslovakia on our long journey to Australia.

My mother was now in an advanced state of dementia and it saddened me that on my return to Australia I would be unable to tell her of the roots trip I had taken with my family. I wondered though what she would have said if she were able to understand me. I think she would have said to me: 'Palko, you are meshuge ('crazy' in Yiddish). You have a happy family and have made a good life in Australia – why would you go back to torture yourself?' She would not have approved because after her trip back in 1978 during the communist era, she was bitterly disappointed. But I had to go and see for myself.

Our trip to Eastern Europe was an eye-opener for us. I felt a sense of relief, but by no means closure. I knew that deep in my heart I still had to find out exactly how my father's fatal journey had ended, fifty-one years ago. But I did not know where to begin.

THE TURNING POINT

By 1998 I found myself talking about my past in more detail. A few years earlier I had donated a perpetual prize to the Emanuel School in memory of my father. The 'Eugen Drexler Memorial Prize' given for history in Year 10 became the 'Eugen Drexler Memorial Prize for Excellence in Holocaust Studies'. Michelle was in Year 10 in 1998 and decided to write my life story as part of her Holocaust assignment. Together we explored the history of Europe and Slovakia, which had to be included as part of my story. Her many interviews with me were helpful to both of us as it encouraged me to document my family's past. Her final assignment was a brief story of my life. Michelle's assignment reached the shortlist of winners. She felt very proud of her efforts, as did I.

When Michelle and I were researching in the library of the Sydney Jewish Museum, I mentioned to the librarian that I was a child survivor of Theresienstadt. A few weeks later I was approached by the Museum for any artefacts I may have from Theresienstadt to be included in 'Within the Walls', an exhibition of Theresienstadt Ghetto 1941–45 which was to open in December 1998. This was not a problem as I had already shown the various items I had from Theresienstadt to the Emanuel School students.

When the exhibition opened I was moved to see in the glass panel titled 'Children of Theresienstadt' my identity card, vaccination card, ration cards and liberation document which I had loaned to the Museum for the exhibition. This exhibition was so successful that in the year 2000 it travelled to Australia's capital, Canberra, and was shown in Old Parliament House. For the exhibition I had also found my childhood blanket, which travelled my life span from six years of age, through the Holocaust and which was then used by my elder daughter, Julie, at pre-school. The Museum's curator, Jane Wesley, was keen to include my blanket in the display in Canberra. Diane and I went to see the exhibition. We were pleased to see the blanket in a separate glass case together with its story and photographs of myself at five years of age, of my mother and me shortly after our arrival in Australia, and of my daughters and me when Julie was three years old, the age when she used the blanket.

This was a turning point in my life. It made me realise that, as a child survivor, I was now among the youngest survivors in Sydney. I now felt committed to take part in the work of the Museum. The Sydney Jewish Museum is a unique institution as it is involved in educating people about the history of the Holocaust, Australian Jewish history and Jewish culture and religion. One of its main aims is teaching tolerance within our society. Many of the guides at the Museum are survivors of the Holocaust, which has a great impact on visitors to the Museum, particularly school groups, as the guides tell their life story during the tour. Diane and I enrolled in a six-month guiding course that was introduced at the Museum in March 2000. We attended the weekly lectures, which broadened our knowledge of the history of the Holocaust. I remember how nervous I was the first time I guided a group of fifteen Year 10 students. Now, ten years later, I am perfectly at ease when I guide either adults or students and tell my life story. The more guiding I do, the more I feel committed to the Sydney Jewish Museum. I consider it of the greatest importance to teach the community about the tragedy of the past and the importance of tolerance.

I joined the Board of the Museum in November 2002 and was the Honorary Treasurer for two years, between 2004 and 2006. I have the utmost respect for all the survivors who have been working in a voluntary capacity since the Museum's inception in 1992. They are the backbone of the Museum.

As I am one of the youngest survivors I feel a tremendous responsibility to educate both young and old about the Holocaust. But each time I tell my life story, a feeling of great sadness comes over me, especially when one of the students asks: 'what happened to your father?'.

THE ONE-OFF LETTER

Exactly twelve months after 'Within the Walls' was shown in Old Parliament House, I received the following letter from Patricia Gorman, dated 21 June 2001.

Dear Mr Drexler

This is a long shot. A year ago I visited 'Within The Walls Theresienstadt Ghetto', at Old Parliament House in Canberra. I had a particular interest in the exhibition as an uncle of mine, Paul Fodor, was incarcerated there – but managed to survive.

In walking around the exhibition I was particularly drawn to a number of exhibits, which derive from the experiences of you and your family. We share the same family name of Drexler. I was born Patricia Drexler in Oxford, England in 1944, the daughter of Slovak Jewish refugees.

As I understand the family name of Drexler is not common in Central Europe, I wonder if there is a chance that we are distantly related?

I recently had a visit from a cousin, who has become interested in the family tree. Enclosed is a copy of his first draft, which still had significant gaps.

Should you find it of any interest I would be pleased to hear from you.

Yours sincerely,

Patricia Gorman (nee Drexler)

I recognised some of the names on Patricia's family tree, particularly my cousin, the late Rose Etinger (nee Drexler) who had been introduced to my mother and me in the early sixties. Over the years, Rose Etinger had referred to her first cousin George Drexler (George and Patricia's father, Imre Drexler, were brothers) who lived in England and with whom she and her husband, Manek, had visited. I was stunned. The evidence that Patricia supplied showed that she was a relative on my father's side.

I phoned Patricia and we had a long discussion about the family tree she had sent me. Her great-grandfather was born in Špačince, my birthplace and that of my father, grandfather and great-grandfather. Patricia was the eldest of three girls born to Imre and Medy Drexler. I had now found three Drexler cousins: Patricia, Sonja and Elena Drexler.

We made inquiries at the Archives Office in Bratislava. They confirmed that there are positive links between our families. We are third cousins – the only living cousins I have on my father's side.

The warmth that has grown between Patricia's family and mine is so gratifying. Patricia is married to Brian Gorman and they have three adult daughters, Kate, Claire and Sara. They have stayed with us and we have stayed with them at their home on the South Coast of New South Wales. They have greatly enriched our lives. After all these years, relatives on my father's side found me. This was another turning point in my life. If only I could discuss this wonderful news with my mother. And, what would my father have thought?

DEATH OF OUR PARENTS

My mother's condition deteriorated in early 2003. She was sleeping most of the day and was not interested in food. Deep inside of me I had the feeling that my mother had given up the will to live. Her deterioration continued. I found this very difficult to accept, as she was always a real fighter.

I visited my mother at lunchtimes at Montefiore in order to help feed her. Diane and I spent many hours with her with the hope that our presence would encourage her to take some interest in her surroundings and, most importantly, to try to eat a little more. When she developed pneumonia in the first weeks of June, her doctor told us that as she was now in poor health overall and might not recover. It was devastating for me to see her curled up in bed, quite helpless. I wished there was something we could have done.

Diane and I spent her last days at her bedside stroking her hands and talking to her, although we did not know if she could hear our voices. My mother passed away peacefully on Monday 23 June 2003, aged ninety-seven. My mind flashed back to May 1945 when my mother buried her mother in Kolin, on the way home from Theresienstadt. I thought to myself – how did she cope attending to the burial of her mother in an unknown place?

I travelled a long and hard road with my mother and I still feel that she is a part of me and watches over me. I can still picture her saying: 'Palko, we did alright for two refugees who arrived in a new land with less than nothing'.

My mother's death came only four months after Diane's father, Howard, had died from acute leukaemia. He was eighty-nine years old. Julie and Michelle had lost their grandparents within months of each other. Diane and I mourned the loss of our remaining parents together. Our immediate family of six was suddenly reduced to four.

We were blessed with tremendous support from our extended family and friends throughout this difficult time in our lives. Howard is buried in the plot he had reserved next to his wife, Cara Esther (Diane's mother) while my mother is buried in a plot we had reserved close by. Their graves are in the Jewish Section of the Macquarie Park Cemetery, Ryde. We held a joint consecration of their tombstones in March 2004 and again we were greatly supported by family and friends. On Diane's initiative we incorporated a tribute to my father on my mother's tombstone.

Rabbi Mendel Kastel from the Great Synagogue, who officiated at Howard and Helen's funerals and their consecrations, gave the four of us tremendous support throughout our bereavements. He also consecrated the tribute in memory of my father. I felt very emotional saying Kaddish for my father. My thoughts went back to my childhood, remembering the happy times with him, and although I did not know where he was buried I now had a memorial to him, which gave me some satisfaction. However, deep in my heart I knew I had to find my father's final resting place.

1   It is customary to light a candle on the anniversary of the death of a loved one. The candle, which is specially mounted in a tin container, burns for 24 hours. A candle is also lit on Yom Kippur, the holiest day in the Jewish calendar, when there is a memorial service for all those who have died. These candles are normally lit in the home.

2   Kaddish is a prayer which is said in memory of relatives, friends and fellow Jewish people who have passed away.

3   From 'A Look Back Over my Shoulder' by Garry Fabian 2002. I met Garry, also a child survivor, of Theresienstadt in 2003. As he is four years older than I, he was more aware of what was said and what happened in Theresienstadt.

4   'Jewish Prague' by Marie Vitochova 1995.

CHAPTER
VII

JOURNEY OF DISCOVERY

While I was sitting Shiva[1] at home for my mother, I spent a lot of time thinking about my parents and the short but precious years we were a family. I had just buried my mother but I had no knowledge of where my father was buried. It consumed me; I needed to know where his final resting place was. When I finally came out of my state of reflection I said to Diane, 'I must go to Lübeck, Germany'.

Back in 2000 I had thought about my father's death and had written to the Mayor of Lübeck, inquiring as to whether there was a memorial to the prisoners killed on 3 May 1945 in Lübeck Bay. I also asked if there was a record of those who died and/or a burial site. He replied promptly, and sent a copy of an article *The Cap Arcona Disaster on 3 May 1945* as well as photocopies of various memorials in the Lübeck area pertaining to the disaster. As the information was in German, I asked Diane's father, Howard, if he would translate it. I was dumbfounded when he read me the translation. I had no idea that there were three ships involved and that the British Air Force had killed over 10,000 prisoners in a one-day bombing mission on 3 May 1945.

My daughter Julie saw how disturbed I was then and wanted to help me come to grips with the information. She spent many hours on the internet researching the disaster. The information she found was absolutely astounding. I could not believe that such an event took place five days before the Germans surrendered to the Allies.

After my mother died in June 2003 I found myself unable to cope with this discovery, so I tried to put the matter aside. I became extremely angry. Then guilt took over from anger. I began to think irrationally and continually blamed myself for not having made inquires earlier when my mother may have been able to assist and we could have gone to Lübeck together. I repeatedly dreamt about my father getting off the bus with my mother in Špačince in 1945. In my dreams he was wearing the same grey pants, jacket and cap that he wore when I last saw him in Sered in December 1944. He had returned after all! Then I would wake up, my body covered in perspiration. My dreams propelled me to make the decision: I needed to go to the area and stand on the soil where my father was killed. I needed to uncover the missing pieces surrounding his death.

I became obsessed with finding the truth about my father's death. Not one day would go by without me thinking about his torment in the bombing mission perpetrated by the British. I thought about it during my waking hours and could not comprehend why and how my father got to northern Germany. At night I tossed and turned and feared of dreaming again of transports of striped uniformed men crowded in cattle trains. I carried out extensive research on the disaster in Lübeck Bay that occurred in May 1945 and felt more confident to plan a visit there in May 2004.

First I telephoned the Jewish Community Centre in Lübeck and eventually spoke to Cantor Chaim Kornblum. On his suggestion I faxed him the details I had relating to my father's death. Cantor Kornblum forwarded my fax to Dr Ingeburg Klatt, Director of the Lübeck Cultural Centre. Dr Klatt was responsible for cultural affairs in the Lübeck area. She had gained her doctorate researching post World War II life in Germany and had been responsible for several exhibitions of Jewish life before and after 1945. She responded to me by email, strongly suggesting that we should plan to be there for the yearly commemoration at the Memorial in Neustadt in Holstein on 3 May 2004.

Unfortunately she would be unable to attend this commemoration but she offered to take us the next day to the commemoration of the boats going to the area where the *Cap Arcona* and *Thielbek* were sunk. We accepted her kind invitation.

On 1 May 2004 Diane and I left Sydney, travelling by plane to Frankfurt, then to Hamburg and lastly by train to Lübeck – a total of thirty hours. We arrived in Lübeck in the afternoon of Sunday 2 May.

Lübeck is a beautiful mediaeval town in the very north of Germany. It is a large Baltic port and sits on the River Trave which flows into Lübeck Bay. We were to attend the memorial service on 3 May at Neustadt on the Baltic Sea, thirty-two kilometres north of Lübeck. I telephoned Cantor Kornblum on the Sunday to clarify if he would be going to the service. He told me that the Jewish Community had conducted its own memorial service that morning so he would not be attending.

At 8.30 am on Monday 3 May we left Lübeck by train for Neustadt to attend the 10 am service. It was cold, rainy and very miserable, but considering the solemnity of the occasion, the weather was appropriate. We took a taxi from the station to the memorial site. The service was held at the memorial built to commemorate the disaster, on top of the hill, in alignment with the position at sea where the ships sank. There were about thirty people gathered there. At exactly 10 am, a distinguished looking man with a beard and dressed as a sea captain approached the dais. At the same time several men walked to the memorial in regimental style, each with a huge wreath of flowers, which they laid in a ceremonial formation. The man on the dais began his speech, in German, recalling the bombing and shipping disaster of 3 May 1945. He ended by stating that a disaster like this should never have happened and should never happen again in the world.

I had never felt more miserable in my life. More than 10,000 human beings died on that day, my father among them. Yet this man spoke without emotion. He merely gave an account of yet another disaster of the war. We found the service sterile; not even a single prayer uttered.

At the conclusion of the service I approached the speaker and introduced myself. He explained that he was the Mayor of Neustadt and that most of the people at the service were residents of the area. He introduced me to Wilhelm Lange, an interesting man in his mid-forties whose mission was to keep the memory of the disaster alive and to educate the next generation. He was a teacher, historian and director of the Cap Arcona Museum in Neustadt. He had written several books about the disaster and was passionate about the subject. On my introduction, he immediately said in English: 'Mr Drexler, you have been announced by Dr Klatt from the Lübeck Cultural Centre'. From the very beginning Lange was extremely attentive and became our host guide. He introduced me to the only survivor present at the service: Fritz Bringmann, aged eighty-two, a German who had been a political prisoner held at Neuengamme. He was not on the ships.

I was very impressed by Lange. He was passionate about the history of this disaster and felt it his 'duty' to tell me everything he could. On leaving the memorial, Herr Lange took us to the Jewish Cemetery where there is a mass grave and memorial to the dead prisoners found on the beaches. The headstone on the mass grave reads:

> Those buried in this place died in Neustadt on
> and after the day of Liberation May 3, 1945.

As I stood there in the rain, mesmerised by the graves around me, I could only direct my thoughts to my father. A gentle, good man from Špačince, loved by his family and friends, and respected by all the farmers in the district where he lived; and a victim of a tyrant's war.

Was he buried in this mass grave or one of the fourteen cemeteries along the bay of Lübeck?

The rain continued to fall as I stood there reciting Kaddish for my father. Herr Lange waited patiently in the rain while Diane and I paid our homage in the cemetery.

Lange ushered us to his car and took us to the Cap Arcona Museum in the township. As the director of this museum, he was eager to give us a personal guided tour. On display were photographs and memorabilia from the *Cap Arcona*, and a written history of the ship.

By now it was mid-afternoon. Herr Lange invited us to return to Neustadt the following day to participate in the tribute to the prisoners who died on the ships, that takes place at sea near the position where the boats actually sank.

On the train back to Lübeck, Diane and I discussed our extraordinary day. My confrontation with the past had left me upset and angry. I couldn't imagine having gone through this day alone – Diane's support gave me strength to carry on. Later that afternoon when we returned to the Alter Speicher Hotel in Lübeck, I wanted to rest but could not. My adrenaline was pumping fast. I needed to walk the streets and my anger increased as I walked. I did not know where I was going. I passed the tourist mall and kept walking and walking. I must have walked for about two hours before returning to the hotel.

Dr Klatt picked us up from our hotel mid-morning the next day. It was another cold, wet, miserable, foggy day. En route to Neustadt, she took us to the Vorwerker Industriehafen (shipping docks) in Lübeck where concentration camp prisoners were boarded on to the Athen and ferried out to the *Cap Arcona* and *Thielbek*. I could not control my heartbeat when she pointed out a copper plaque on the side on the docks, which had been erected in tribute to the 8000 prisoners who died at sea on 3 May 1945. The sheer horror of what had occurred here was becoming more and more real to me.

On our arrival in Neustadt, we joined Herr Lange and a group of young adult teachers who were interested in World War II history. We proceeded to the navy docks and our group of fifteen boarded a navy boat. This was the site of a submarine training station and the same area where German crews were trained for the U-boats during World War II.

Our boat sailed to the area where the *Cap Arcona* sank, four kilometres from shore. There, we scattered flowers on the sea in tribute to the dead. Throughout the journey Herr Lange talked about the incident. He explained to the history teachers that the largest ship, *Cap Arcona*, had explosives in its bows, deliberately put there by the Nazis so that when hit by the British, the whole ship would explode. There was a Scandinavian man in our party who was very emotional and told us his story. In May 1945 he was nine years old and lived with his family in Neustadt. He recalled how they heard the explosion and saw the smoke rising from the *Cap Arcona*. He had never seen such a sight and was very scared. For the next day and many weeks thereafter, he and his family, including his four year old sister, went down to the beach and watched the waterlogged bodies

Martyrs' Memorial outside the Status Quo Temple, Trnava.
Photo taken in 1996.

Outside the apartment in Trnava where I lived with my mother, 1946–47. Photo taken in 1996.

The street in Trnava where we lived. The entrance to the apartments is next to the RHS Lekaren (pharmacy).

Photo taken 1996.

Top: *Standing in front of the Hamburg Barracks, where I stood many times as a child in 1944–45.*

Bottom: *Hamburg Barracks in Terezín. Photos taken in 2004.*

Top: *Memorial on the beach at Neustadt in Holstein for all the victims of the 3 May 1945 disaster. Photo taken in May 2004.*

Bottom: *Cap Arcona on fire, 3 May 1945.*

Gerry Brent, 1945.

My Repatriation registration certificate.

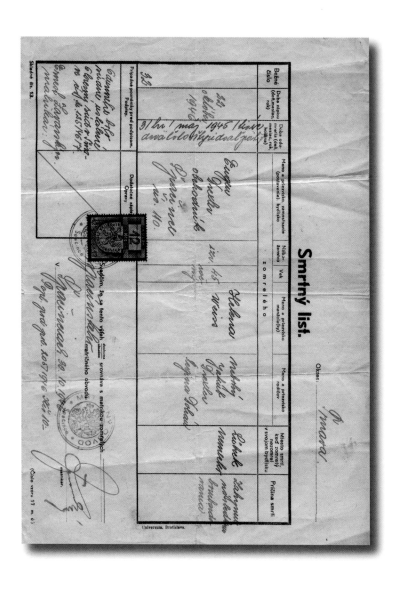

The original death certificate of my father, Eugen Drexler, 1945.

wash ashore. He could not forget this sight. It gave him and his sister nightmares for a long time. He said he needed to attend the memorial and obtain confirmation of his memories. This was the first time he had returned to his home town to seek the truth.

Back at the navy docks our whole group went to the Cap Arcona Museum where Herr Lange showed us a film about the disaster made by BBC Television[2]. He also provided a commentary, giving further explanations to events of that fateful day. Dr Klatt, like the rest of us, was very impressed with Herr Lange's exposition.

I left there with mixed emotions: angry with the Germans for killing the Jews, and angry with the British for their disregard of the innocent and their overriding desire for a final air conquest at the end of the war. If only the British had accepted the surrender of the Germans for Northern Germany in the morning of 3 May 1945, the lives of more than 10,000 people could have been saved. My father would not have been killed.

My mind was saturated with the events of the biggest sea disaster and the unforgettable tragedy of that day. I had stood on the soil where my father was killed; I had attended a memorial service and had said Kaddish. However, I still had no idea of the movements of my father after he left Sered. How did he get to Lübeck Bay? Which concentration camp or camps was he in after Sered? Was he on a death march? My mind was full with unanswered questions. One thing I did know was that I had to find out. I needed the answers.

DISASTER AT LÜBECK BAY

As I discovered during my extensive research, by January 1945 it was obvious that Germany had lost the war. Right up to the end of the war the Germans tried to hide the horror of the concentration camps from the world. It was clear that they did not want a single prisoner to escape. As the allies were advancing in Germany, the SS closed slave labour camps, destroyed records and dispatched able prisoners further north on death marches. Prisoners who were too sick or too weak to march were shot.

Most of the prisoners who were killed at Lübeck Bay on 3 May 1945 were from Neuengamme. As my father had been killed in the bombardment I thought it a strong possibility that he was transferred from Neuengamme to Lübeck Bay.

Neuengamme was the largest concentration camp in Northern Germany, located about twenty kilometres northeast of Hamburg. It had ninety satellite camps under its control. Himmler issued orders to the commanders of Neuengamme concentration camp that surrender was unacceptable, and so the closing down of the camp complex began on 24 March 1945 with the clearance of the satellite camps. During the clearance the SS crammed up to 100 prisoners into each freight carriage. On these transports, which took over a week, the prisoners were given little or no food or water.

Many prisoners died of starvation or disease and were buried beside the tracks. When transport by rail was not possible, the prisoners were herded out of the camp on foot. These torturous marches lasted days, sometimes weeks. The prisoners were given no provisions or footwear. The guards shot those who collapsed or could not keep up. Roughly fifty per cent of the prisoners did not survive the journey.[3]

As the death marches advanced northwards of Hamburg, Gaulieter Karl Kaufmann decided to load the prisoners onto ships, send the ships out to sea and then sink them in order to remove any witnesses. There were few remaining ships and ferries in the area, with most already deployed in the East to rescue civilians and retreating German troops who were fleeing the Russians, but Kaufmann had the authority to requisition non-military vessels.

He chose his three ships. The 27,500 ton passenger liner *Cap Arcona* and the 2800 ton freighter *Thielbek* were anchored in Lübeck Bay, offshore from Neustadt. The 10,000 ton *Athen* was in Neustadt harbour. The first Neuengamme concentration camp inmates arrived in cattle wagons at Lübeck harbour on 19 April 1945. From 19 to 26 April further transports arrived. The prisoners were loaded onto the ships. There were no toilets, food or water, and each day prisoners died by the hundreds, their bodies causing stench and disease that prompted even more deaths among the half-starved thousands that remained.

By May 1945 the death marches had claimed thousands of victims. Himmler's orders not to leave witnesses for the oncoming Allies showed the sheer desperation of the Nazi leadership towards the end of the war.

After Hitler's suicide on 30 April, Neuengamme concentration camp Commandant Max Pauly conceived a treacherous trap for the RAF. Under his instruction, it was falsely reported that the German leadership planned to leave for Norway and continue to fight on from there – the Germans wanted the British to believe that the three ships in Lübeck Bay were full of SS escaping to Norway. On 2 May the British reconnaissance spotted the ships together with destroyers and some U-boats in the area. They fell for the trap. That same day the last prisoners were ferried from the Lübeck docks. Later in the day the British Army liberated Lübeck City.

On the morning of 3 May 1945, Dr Arnoldson, the Swedish Red Cross representative based in Lübeck, informed British Headquarters that he had received information that there would be air raids over Lübeck Bay, which would expose three ships crowded with prisoners to grave danger. Unfortunately, this information was not transmitted to the RAF squadrons in time. On the first clear day, 3 May 1945, at 2 pm, four squadrons of British Typhoons carrying rockets and bombs, attacked the ships. The *Thielbek* sank immediately with about 2800 prisoners on board while the *Cap Arcona* with at least 5000 prisoners on board was ablaze. The *Athen*, with 2000 prisoners on board was alongside the quay of the naval base. Miraculously, no-one on the *Athen* was killed. During these raids U-boats in the harbour and other warships were also hit. The combination of these deadly weapons and the cold Baltic Sea meant that there was very little chance of prisoners surviving.

The British – the liberators – unintentionally became the killers of thousands of desperate prisoners. The Germans shot the prisoners still stranded on the beach.

Fishing boats picked up some prisoners.[4] There were 50 survivors from the *Thielbek* and 350 from the *Cap Arcona*, but 8000 had already died on those two ships, and 2000 died on the beaches.

At around 4 pm the same day the British marched into Neustadt; they found that the Germans had fled – there was no resistance. On 4 May 1945, Field Marshall Montgomery, Commander in Chief of the British Forces, accepted surrender from the Germans in the north. Four days later, on 8 May 1945, Germany surrendered. The war in Europe was over.

The British appointed a war crimes investigation team to investigate the disaster at Lübeck Bay. Major Noel O'Till, the team leader, submitted his report in July 1945. The conclusion of the investigation was simple. The SS were ultimately responsible for the disaster. RAF intelligence officers were also blamed. They failed to pass on to the pilots information that there had been prisoners on the ships.[5] The RAF has classified the full transcripts of the investigation – not to be released until 2045.

GERMANY AND THE CZECH REPUBLIC, MAY 2004

Our four-day mission in Lübeck Bay left us feeling totally unreal, as if in a 'Kafka' dream. On the fifth day we travelled by train to Hamburg, one hour south of Lübeck. We visited Neuengamme Concentration Camp Memorial, twenty kilometres east of Hamburg. I thought there was a strong possibility that my father may have been imprisoned there in early 1945 before being transferred to Lübeck Bay; hence my need to visit this well known hell hole.

Neuengamme was opened in 1938 as an extension of Sachsenhausen Concentration Camp. In 1940 it became independent and a brick factory was established and run by the SS in the camp. Neuengamme was known for the extreme cruelty and sadism inflicted by the SS and their appointed Kapos, hardened German criminals. The SS set up this camp for the purpose of 'extermination through work'.

The largest numbers of prisoners were from the Soviet Union (34,000), followed by Poland (17,000) and France (11,500). An estimated 55,000 of the total of 106,000 prisoners (which included 13,000 women) died as a result of SS brutality and the severe living and working conditions.

Most of the inmates were political prisoners, but most of the 9000 German prisoners in Neuengamme were professional criminals. There were also gypsies, homosexuals and Jehovah's Witnesses imprisoned in Neuengamme. Only 13,000 Jews were imprisoned in Neuengamme, mainly during the last two years of the war, when Jews were transferred from Auschwitz as slave labour for the armament industry in one of Neuengamme's satellite camps. The Jews were treated appallingly by the SS and most died as a result of work and camp conditions. SS doctors used lethal injections to kill 'useless' prisoners suffering from TB and malnutrition. These doctors also conducted inhumane medical experiments on ill and healthy prisoners, both adults and children.

It was cold, foggy and miserable as Diane and I set out from Hamburg by train and bus to Neuengamme. We were greeted by an oppressive sight. The memorial is spread out over a huge area. There are fifteen buildings in their original state as well as The House of Commemoration on whose walls are listed names of prisoners who died there. It took us fifteen minutes to walk from the House of Commemoration to the archives building. I was hoping to find my father's name in the archives, but it was not there. The registrar told me that before the evacuation of the camp in 1945 the SS destroyed half the records. I felt weak at the knees and had to sit down. Diane quickly went into her bag and brought out the bottle of water for me, and after a few minutes I regained my composure. My thoughts were with my father's plight if he were imprisoned in this cruel place.

From here we walked to the main museum building, passing former prisoner barracks, the brick factory and various remnants of carriages and implements used for the transport of the bricks. The impact of the exhibits titled 'The Fight to Survive' in the main exhibition hall leaves one with a powerful message of the prisoners' desperation. Seeing the prisoners' bunks with their bare timber boards together with large photographs of men standing in a role call in freezing conditions made me tremble. I was hoping that my father was never in Neuengamme.

Interestingly, the only other people we saw during our three hours at Neuengamme were groups of students with their teachers. No sane person would want to visit here and traipse through the long grass and swamps as we did. I was beginning to wonder if I was sane. As we walked back along the road to the bus stop I kept repeating to Diane that I thought it must have been one of the closest places to hell. If only I knew the route my father would have been marched along after he left Sered and at which camp he would have been imprisoned en route to Lübeck Bay. I felt totally empty inside. Thank goodness I had Diane with me as my support.

That Friday evening, we attended the Shabbat service at the Hamburg Synagogue. I quietly said Kaddish for all those who lost their lives in Neuengamme and for my father, yet again. Every time I heard mention of Berlin, I recoiled from the face of Nazism it represented to me. It scared me. However, when we were planning this mission, friends suggested we include Berlin in our itinerary. They said that since the destruction of the Wall, Berlin had become the city of the memory of the Holocaust. I became increasingly curious and as we were in Germany, it would be opportune to visit. As well, Diane's father had lived in Berlin for some years prior to his departure for Australia in 1938. So, we went to Berlin.

I was pleasantly surprised. It was a very friendly city to visit; English was spoken wherever we went. We stayed in a boutique hotel in the former East Germany. They have been and still are restoring the beautiful buildings. We were so fortunate to have Erika Falkenreck, a retired historian and lecturer at the university, as our guide. She literally took us everywhere. Erika felt it her duty to make amends for the sins of the past. She had a wealth of knowledge and was sympathetic to the vast number of memorials to the Holocaust that have been prominently erected in the city and other outlying districts of Berlin. We ambled for hours in the old Jewish area where the buildings have been restored since the end of communism. The shell of the Berlin Synagogue in Orianbergstrasse still stands, in all its grandeur, as a museum. We spent one full afternoon going through the Berlin Jewish Museum, designed by architect Daniel Libeskind. It displays the origins, traditions and history of Germany Jewry. The message I came away with was that the Jewish people were prominent in every aspect of German society over many centuries. Why then, did this German cultured society support the elimination of the Jewish race?

Our next city was Prague. As we had been there in 1996, and felt very much at ease there, this visit was like coming home. The main purpose of going back to Prague was my need to visit Terezín again. I needed to walk the streets, smell the air, and in my own way hopefully come to terms with that time of my life. I had made an appointment with the Director of the Terezín Ghetto Museum before we left Sydney, as I needed to get confirmation of some memories that were puzzling me. Dr Blodig was very hospitable to us and put my mind at ease. He tried to help me trace records of prisoners from Sered to their destinations. Unfortunately all had been destroyed.

Since our visit eight years ago, there had been an overwhelming revitalisation of the exhibition area. An additional exhibition in the refurbished Magdeburg Barracks had been opened. The exhibitions in the Magdeburg Barracks illustrate largely the art and culture that existed in Theresienstadt during those cold days of World War II. What took me by surprise was the recreation of a dormitory similar to the one my mother and I lived in inside the Hamburg Barracks. For a split second I froze. Suddenly I was back in the years 1944–45. The past flashed in front of me like a nightmare.

As I walked the streets of Terezín I tried to reflect on the times I had walked there during my imprisonment. Nothing had changed. It was cold and miserable fifty-nine years ago, eight years ago when I took my family, and today; everything was the same. I stood outside the gate of the Hamburg Barracks as I had done many times when I was six years of age. Back then there was activity in the street; today no-one was there except Diane and me. Standing there, I thought of my loving mother and the many sacrifices she made to save my life.

As we boarded the bus to take us back to Prague I said to myself: 'I have been to Terezín three times in my life. I will never return'.

We had now been travelling two and a half weeks, all of which had been centred on research about what had happened to my family. I had stood on the beach where my father had died. I had learnt from residents and historians how the disaster at Lübeck Bay came about. I had a deeper understanding of the last major disaster perpetrated in World War II. And yet, my questions had not all been answered; I still did not know how my father came to be at Lübeck Bay, or where he was buried.

LÜBECK POSTSCRIPT

On my return to Sydney in June 2004 I experienced an amazing coincidence. This is something I still find hard to believe. I was telling a client about my trip and my need to research the death of my father on 3 May 1945 at Lübeck Bay. He suddenly retorted, 'I was there on that day'. I was speechless. My client, Gerry Brent, was a Second Lieutenant in the British No. 6 Army Commando, which arrived in Neustadt in the afternoon of 3 May, in time to see the result of the huge disaster.

As an eighteen year old Jewish boy living in Germany in 1938, Gerry lived in an atmosphere of uncertainty. In September 1938 the German government ordered Jews to present their passports at the immigration office for stamping with a large red 'J'. The idea originated in Switzerland where Swiss authorities were anxious to stop the flow of German Jews trying to enter the country. The day before they had to surrender them, Gerry's father urged him to get out of Berlin while he still had a 'clean' passport. Gerry headed to Denmark and was able to stay with a friend until he received a visa to enter England. His brother was already in England and his parents were fortunate enough to leave on the last ship out of Germany sailing to England in 1939.

Gerry studied aeronautical engineering at the Royal Aeronautical College London until 1940, when he was classed as an 'Enemy Alien Class B' and interned after Dunkirk and sent to Canada. As an enemy alien he was forced to stay for a year behind barbed wire in New Brunswick, Frederickton, Canada. In July 1941 he returned to England to complete his engineering course. Later that year, he joined the British Army Pioneer Corp and was stationed at Pembroke Docks, Wales. At the end of 1942 the government decided that Jews in the British Army could fight as regular troops. He was placed in the Royal Electrical & Mechanical Engineers.

In the winter of 1943 Gerry attended an officer-training course and became a Second Lieutenant[6], joining the Forty-seventh Royal Marine Commando Unit, who fought in Holland in late 1944. In January 1945 he returned to England and was transferred to No. 6 Army Commando, which was posted to Germany. He fought at the crossing of the Elbe, the last river to be crossed before entering Hamburg. From there his unit was among the forces that proceeded north and liberated Neustadt. Gerry became very emotional as he told me that he saw bodies of prisoners spread across the beaches and docks. Many had been shot while others had been clubbed to death with rifle butts. He admitted that it was the most gruesome sight of his entire war experience. It was a scene of a slaughterhouse. The Nazis had all disappeared. A small number of surviving prisoners were wandering around like zombies. Many did not know what had happened to them.

Gerry's unit rounded up German residents of Neustadt and took them down to the beaches where they were given shovels and spades to dig ditches in the sand and bury the dead. As the tide went out, the bodies originally buried in the sand were collected and buried in the various cemeteries in the Neustadt area.

What an extraordinary link I now had between my father and Gerry. It had come out of the blue, in the most unexpected way. This man, sitting opposite me, had witnessed the conditions in which my father had been killed. He had been there. Was my father's body among those buried on the beach?

MOMENT OF TRUTH

It was now August 2004. I had now spent the last two years researching my father's movements between Sered and Lübeck Bay, his place of death on 3 May 1945. As well as travelling to Lübeck in May, I had spent countless hours researching on the internet and reading as much as I could find. In addition, Professor Konrad Kwiet, Resident Historian at the Sydney Jewish Museum, gave me contacts to his colleagues at the Washington Holocaust Museum, archives and historians in Bratislava, and the Terezín Institute. I also researched the archives at the Jewish Holocaust Museum and Research Centre in Melbourne as well as Yad Vashem Israel, just to mention a few, but nothing positive came my way. I was now totally frustrated. I had come to the end of the road. I was very angry with myself. Why hadn't I done something about this earlier?

The breakthrough happened in October 2004. It started when Diane's cousin, Bev Cohen from Melbourne, sent me a circular she had received from the Jewish Museum in Melbourne advertising that Oz Opera, as part of the Melbourne International Arts Festival, would be presenting the children's opera Brundibar by Hans Krasa in November. This children's opera was staged fifty-five times in Theresienstadt during World War II.

Following this, Mim Segal, Bev's sister, sent me a newspaper cutting from *The Age* newspaper, dated

3 November 2004 and titled 'For a boy interned in a Nazi concentration camp, joining the opera proved a gift of life'. This article appeared as publicity for the forthcoming production of the opera Brundibar, focusing on the life of a seven year old boy, Peter Gaspar, who arrived in Theresienstadt in January 1945 and appeared in a production. The article also stated that Peter and his mother were liberated in Theresienstadt and were reunited in Bratislava, Slovakia, in June 1945 with his father who had survived slave labour camps and death marches.

This small piece of information was of huge importance to me. My heart was pounding as I read this article over and over again. I wanted to speak to Peter Gaspar as soon as possible. Fortunately, Bev knew him and was able to get his telephone number. I was concerned as to what Peter's reaction might be, receiving a call from a stranger inquiring into his family's past. I calmed myself and telephoned him.

Once I had gone through all the preliminaries, I could feel that Peter was willing to share his experience and knowledge with me. We established that he and his mother left Sered on 16 January 1945 on Transport no. XXVI/2, arriving in Theresienstadt on 19 January 1945. My mother and I had been on the previous transport – no. XXVI/1, which left Sered on 19 December 1944 and arrived at Theresienstadt four days later. On arrival at Theresienstadt, Peter was placed in the Boys' Home where I was living, at 17 Hauptstrasse. Unlike me, Peter lived in the Boys' Home until liberation.

I asked him what details he knew about the slave labour camps and the death marches his father was on. He was hesitant in his reply, but went on to reveal to me that his father had been put on a transport of men only, which had left Sered on 16 January 1945, and was sent to Germany. His father was liberated in Lübeck. I felt all my blood rushing to my heart. Could my father have been on the same transport? If so, how did Peter's father survive and mine not?

The following day Peter rang me. He said he had remembered that he had a 1945 Slovak diary and a small notebook that his father had written in during his imprisonment from January 1945 to liberation.

He said he found it hard to decipher both the diary and the notebook as they were written in Slovak; however, he was able to translate a few details which he read out to me. 'Departed Sered 16 January 1945; arrived Sachsenhausen 20 January; arrived Wittstock 25 April; liberated at Lübeck May 1945'. Peter's father, Imre, died in 1983 and his mother, Jenny, died in 1996, both in Melbourne.

I found myself trembling and for about a minute was speechless. I already knew from my research that only one transport of men left Sered at around this time. Therefore, Peter's father and my father must have been on the same trasport. I now knew the date that my father left Sered, and where his transport was heading. This was the missing link for which I had been searching for over two years. I could not believe that I had searched all over the world for this information and by pure luck the information was in a diary and notebook that had survived the Holocaust and was in Melbourne! I was anxious to meet Peter and read his father's diary notes for myself.

Our trip to Melbourne was memorable. Not only did I meet Peter Gaspar, a fellow child survivor of Theresienstadt, but for the first time I was able to read original evidence of the greatest importance to my long search.

I am convinced that my father and Peter's father were on the same transport of men sent on 16 January 1945 from Sered to the barbaric forced labour camp of Sachsenhausen, thirty-five kilometres north of Berlin. All the evidence links together: the dates in Peter's father's diary matched the departure date of my father from Sered; the man at Bratislava train station who had given my mother the news of my father's death had told her that he and my father were subjected to hard labour for a long time, followed by a march to Lübeck Bay, where my father was killed on the beach; and my research revealed that thousands of prisoners were killed during the death marches following the evacuation of Sachsenhausen in April 1945. As the Red Army was approaching Sachenhausen, the stronger prisoners were marched further north to the Baltic Sea to join up with the floating concentration camps in Lübeck Harbour.

On the torturous death marches the prisoners weaved their way through forests to avoid the British and American armies. According to Imre Gaspar's notes, all the nights were spent in the forests. The prisoners were short of rations. One night he ate horsemeat and another night one spoon of flour. From the available evidence, I now believe that my father was among the prisoners who reached Lübeck Bay on foot on 3 May 1945. As he British bombardment had started it was too late for the group in which my father was to be put on board the *Cap Arcona* or the *Thielbek*.

The prisoners thought they would live and return to their homes and their loved ones. However, the SS, in a final act of barbarism, deceived these helpless, emaciated men, who were hungry and thirsty, into believing that they were to board Red Cross ships which would take them to safety. Only a few of the prisoners managed to escape the slaughter, Peter's father among them. On the beach at Neustadt, the SS, German marines and the Hitler Youth were all desperate to kill as many of the prisoners as they could in their final act of murder. The prisoners were machine-gunned to death. In addition to the 8000 prisoners bombed and rocketed on the two ships, about another 2000 were massacred on the beaches. If my father was with the same group of men as Peter's, as I believe he was, then he was one of the 2000. He died only a few hours before the liberation of Neustadt.

As I was about to be set free from Theresienstadt, my father was over 1200 kilometres away in Lübeck Bay, Germany. On 3 May 1945 he thought, so I believe, that he was to go to a Red Cross ship and to freedom; but instead he was killed – murdered in a final act of German bastardry – on the sands of that lonely beach. His death and those of several hundred other Jews was a desperate act by the killers to leave no witnesses to the 'Final Solution' to the 'Jewish Question'.

I feel sure that this is how he died, but I gain no solace knowing this. I have searched for him and the truth. I still do not have closure. But what my journey has done is to bring his memory to life for me, as well as for Diane, Julie and Michelle. In that way, I have been able to reclaim my father.

His being has left an indelible mark on me. My father, Eugen Drexler, will always be a part of me and I will always miss him. Each time I visit my mother's grave at the cemetery, I read the memorial on her tombstone dedicated to him:

> In Loving Memory of
> EUGEN DREXLER
> 26 January 1900 – 3 May 1945
> Who Perished in Lübeck, Germany
> A Victim of the Holocaust.

1   Shiva is the week of mourning immediately after the funeral when the bereaved stays at home and is visited by family and friends.

2   BBC, VE-Day Neustadt, Germany, London 1985–95.

3   Lange, Wilhelm: Cap Arcona Das tragische Ende der KZ-Häftlings Flotte am.3. Mai 1945. Dockumentation (3.erw.Aufl.) Eutin 1992.

4   Benjamin Jacobs, *The Dentist of Auschwitz*, University Press Kentucky, 1995

5   Lawrence Bond, *Typhoons' Last Storm* (documentary film), History Channel, 2000

6   This category of second and third rank was given to Jewish soldiers.

APPENDIX

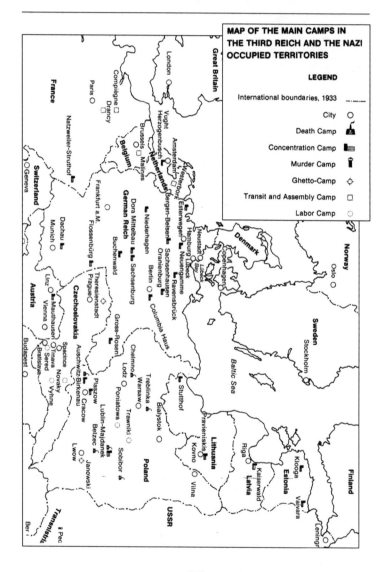

MAP OF THE MAIN CAMPS IN THE THIRD REICH AND THE NAZI OCCUPIED TERRITORIES

LEGEND

International boundaries, 1933	—··—
City	O
Death Camp	
Concentration Camp	
Murder Camp	
Ghetto-Camp	⬦
Transit and Assembly Camp	□
Labor Camp	○

REFERENCES

ARCHIVES

Imperial War Museum Archives No 2, (1945) War Crimes
Investigation Team Reports 19

BOOKS

Blodig V, (2003), *Terezín Litomerice Places of Suffering and Braveness*, The Terezín Memorial, Prague

Bondy R, (1981), *Elder of the Jews Jacob Edelstein*, Grove Press, New York

Chesnoff R, (2000), *Pack of Thieves*, Weidenfeld & Nicolson, London

Fabian G, (2002), *A Look Back Over My Shoulder*, Makor Jewish Community Library, Melbourne

Gilbert M, (1982), *Atlas of the Holocaust*, Michael Joseph Ltd, London

Jacobs B, (1995), *The Dentist of Auschwitz*, University Press, Kentucky

Karas J, (1985), *Music in Terezín 1941–1945*, Beaufort Books Publishers, New York

KZ-Gedenkstatte Neuengamme, (2005), *Die Ausstellungen*, Bremen

Lange W, (1992), Cap Arcona, Eutin

Singer P, (2003), *Pushing Time Away*, Harper Collins, Sydney

Terezín Initiative Foundation, (1996), *Terezín Memorial Book*, Melantrish Publishing House

The Tragedy of Slovak Jews, (1992), Proceedings of the International Symposium, Ministry of Culture of Slovak Republic, Banska Bystrica

MISCELLANEOUS

Blodig V, (1999), *Terezín in the Final Solution of the Jewish Question*, Conference report of The International Scientific Conference

Bond L, (2000), *Typhoon's Last Storm*, Film Documentary

Museum of the History of Hamburg, (2004), Neuengamme Concentration Camp 1938–1945, Brochure

Neuengamme Concentration Camp (1995), *The Fight to Survive*, Memorial Brochure

INTERVIEWS

Blodig V, Director Ghetto Museum Terezín, Terezín, Czech Republic, 17/05/2004

Brent G, Former British Army Commando 1945, Sydney, Australia, 16/6/2004

Gaspar P, Child Survivor Theresienstadt 1945, Melbourne, Australia, 10/11/2004 & 4/4/2005

Hawling M, Survivor Cap Arcona 1945, Sydney, Australia, 19/01/2005

Klatt I., Director Lubeck Cultural Centre, Lubeck, Germany, 4/05/2004

Lange W, Historian, Director Cap Arcona Museum, Neustadt in Holstein, Germany, 3/05/2004 & 4/05/2004

WEBSITES

Benes E, (2005) <www.spartocus.schooolnet.co.uk/ fwwbenes.htm>, Accessed 27/07/05

History of Czechoslovakia, (2005), <http://en.wikipedia.org. wiki/historyofCzechoslovakia>, Accessed 19/07/05

Sachsenhausen Oranienburg Germany, (2004), <www. jewishgen.org/forgottencamps/sachsenhausen.eng. html>, Accessed 28/11/04

Slovak National Uprising, (2005), <http://en.wikipedia.org/ wiki/slovaknationaluprising>, Accessed 19/07/05

Slovakia, (2005), <www.slovakia.org/history6.htm>, Accessed 19/07/05